GANGS OF PUNJAB

Jupinderjit Singh, Deputy Editor at *The Tribune*, Chandigarh, is an award-winning investigative journalist celebrated for his crime reporting. Author of six books—which have been translated into multiple languages—he is best known for *Who Killed Moosewala*? (2023), a bestseller that examines Punjab's deep-rooted violence through the lens of the singer's murder.

A recipient of the prestigious Prem Bhatia Young Journalist Award, he rediscovered Shaheed Bhagat Singh's lost pistol and chronicled the find in a book. A creative spirit, Singh also writes short stories and poetry, and plays competitive chess.

You can connect with him on:

Facebook: https://www.facebook.com/japs99
X: https://x.com/japs99
LinkedIn: https://www.linkedin.com/in/jupinderjit-singh-9204881a/
Instagram: https://www.instagram.com/jupinderjit/

GANGS OF PUNJAB

GUNS, GREED, AND GIRLFRIENDS

Jupinderjit Singh

RUPA

Published by
Rupa Publications India Pvt. Ltd 2026
161-B/4, Gulmohar House,
Yusuf Sarai Community Centre,
New Delhi 110049

Sales centres:
Bengaluru Chennai
Hyderabad Kolkata Mumbai

The views and opinions expressed in this book are the author's own and the facts are as reported by him; these have been verified to the extent possible, and the publishers are not in any way liable for the same.

P-ISBN: 978-93-5352-483-8
E-ISBN: 978-93-5352-951-2

Second impression 2026

10 9 8 7 6 5 4 3 2

Printed in India

Contents

Introduction *vii*

1. Dimpy Chandbhan 1
2. Rocky Fazilka 31
3. Shera Khuban 48
4. Jaipal Bhullar 68
5. Vicky Gounder 99
6. Gurpreet Sekhon 115
7. Ankit Bhadu 128
8. Teja Mehandpuria 145
9. Davinder Bambiha 160
10. Lawrence Bishnoi 182

Epilogue 205

Acknowledgements 209

Bibliography 211

Introduction

I did not set out to write a book on gangsters. But as a journalist in Punjab, I found myself returning to the same grim headlines—day after day, year after year. Stories of young men with guns, of blood spilled on village roads, of families shattered. The faces changed, the names changed, but the pattern remained the same, becoming difficult to ignore.

Punjab today is home to over 500 criminal gangs and modules, with nearly 2,000 active members. Their reach extends far beyond state borders—from the alleys of Moga to the suburbs of Brampton, from Bathinda to California and Melbourne. Director General of Police Gaurav Yadav has publicly stated that between April 2022 and October 2025, Punjab witnessed as many as 324 armed exchanges between police units and criminal gangs. In these encounters, 24 gangsters were neutralized and 515 arrested, while 319 sustained injuries. Tragically, three police officers attained martyrdom in the line of duty and 41 personnel were injured. The numbers speak to both the ferocity of gang violence and the sacrifices made by the Punjab Police in their effort to contain it.

These gangs are no longer just clusters of isolated, local criminals; they are part of a dangerous web that connects the drug trade, extortion rackets, and even terror networks. They have infiltrated the music industry, the liquor business, and the sand mafia. And yet, disturbingly, they are not just feared—they are followed, admired, even idolized.

Why?

Because Punjab has always revered its warriors—*yoddhas* in local parlance—whether Sikh, Hindu, or Muslim, who stood tall in the face of adversity. In a distorted reflection of that legacy, today's gangsters have become new-age outlaws, romanticized on social media, lionized in songs, and followed by thousands. But behind the bravado and the Instagram reels lies a darker truth.

Who are these young men? Why did they choose this path? Were they born criminals—or did we, as a society, fail them?

Gangs of Punjab began with those questions. My investigation into the murder of Sidhu Moosewala—a case that stunned the nation—led me deeper into the world of Punjab's gangsters. I chose 10 of them for this book, not because they were the most notorious, but because their stories reveal something essential about the times we live in. Many were once promising athletes—wrestlers, *kabaddi* players, sprinters. They had talent, ambition, and dreams. But somewhere along the way, they were abandoned—by their families, by the system, by the very institutions that were meant to nurture, protect, and guide them.

None of them turned to crime out of hunger or poverty. They did not pick up the gun because they had no food on the table. They did it for power, for pride, for revenge—and sometimes, simply because no one stopped them. Their descent into this quagmire was not inevitable. It was preventable.

I believe journalism, at its core, should be a search for understanding. If we want to stop the rise of the next Lawrence Bishnoi, we must first understand how he came to be.

The police have their job—to catch, to charge, to prosecute. The courts have theirs—to judge. But what is the role of a journalist? I believe it is to ask the questions no one else will. To go beyond the scene of crime, into childhood, the turning point, the moment of no return. To trace the making—and unmaking—of a human being.

This book is not just about gangsters. It is about the society that creates them, the politics that protects them, and the culture that celebrates them. It is about the women who love them, the families who lose them, and the police officers who chase them—sometimes for years, and at times even to the grave.

Each chapter focuses on one gangster—his rise, his fall, his relationships, and his final reckoning. From the first don, Dimpy Chandbhan, to the most feared name today—Lawrence Bishnoi—this book traces the evolution of Punjab's gangster culture over four decades.

I have tried my best to verify the claims through multiple sources—court records, police files, interrogation reports, news archives, and first-hand interviews with witnesses, officers, families, and even two gangsters who are still alive. Add to that the unnamed sources a journalist depends upon. In places, I have added dramatization for impact. Some stories may overlap or repeat, as the lives and exploits of these gangsters often intersect. Certain incidents also require contextualization, which at times involves revisiting the same details. The chapters can be read independently of one another.

Readers may find the revenge sagas of these gangsters, and the arcs of their lives and loves, no less engaging than *Badlapur* (2015), *Mirzapur* (from 2018), *Khakee* (starting 2025), and the life of Dawood Ibrahim put together.

This is not a book of judgement. It is a book of reckoning—if we do not understand what creates a gangster, we will never be able to stop the creation of the next one.

It is not that Punjab's youth lack the spark of greatness. They have always had it—in their stride, in their spirit. But too often, that spark, that fire has been misdirected. Now, in Shubman Gill, India's newest Test captain, Punjab finds a beacon. Gill hasn't just rewritten cricketing records—he has begun to rewrite the story of an entire region.

His dimples, his disarming smile, his Adonis-like frame and V-shaped athletic build all radiate the pride of a land unfortunately associated more often with gangsters and terrorists than with greatness.

Gill hails from Chak Jaimal Singh Wala, a village tucked away in the semi-arid belt of Fazilka District, a zone long haunted by gang wars, drug smuggling, farmer suicides, and cancer-related deaths. Within a 50-km radius—spanning Fazilka, Muktsar, Moga, and Faridkot—Punjab has birthed some of India's most feared gangsters over the past two decades.

And these were no petty criminals. Lawrence Bishnoi from Dutaranwali, Dimpy Chandbhan—the state's first modern gangster—from Chandbhan, Shera Khuban from Khuban, Rocky from Jhuggian, Vicky Gounder from Sarawan, and Davinder Bambiha from Bambiha village in Moga—all have been classified as 'Category A' gangsters. Ironically, many were landlords possessing vast tracts of land, from 30 to over 100 acres. Some—like Shera, Davinder, and Vicky—were once promising athletes, their bodies honed for competition before fate led them astray.

Against such a backdrop, Gill's rise is more than a sporting triumph—it is a cultural pivot. His success offers a counter-narrative to the stereotype that Punjabi youth are either migrating abroad, addicted to drugs, or drawn into crime.

For years, the youth of this region have been branded

as misled, their image reinforced by films like *Udta Punjab* (2016). But the state was waiting for a new kind of hero—a yoddha who could embody progressive masculinity with humility. Gill has shown what happens when that same energy is channelled positively; with family support and a strong cricketing culture, things can change.

And Gill is not alone. Harmanpreet Kaur, captain of the first Indian women's cricket team to win the One-Day International World Cup, hails from Moga—a district without even a proper cricket ground. Harmanpreet Singh, captain of the men's hockey team, led India to a bronze medal at the 2024 Paris Olympics.

Together, these athletes are reshaping Punjab's narrative—from a land of outlaws to a cradle of champions.

One can't help but wonder: had fate been kinder, had the choices been different, how many of these gangsters might have stood proudly on podiums instead of figuring on the police's 'Most Wanted' lists?

1

Dimpy Chandbhan

AFTER THE SIZZLING HOT SUMMER of May and June in the plains of Punjab, the month of July brings a dip in the temperature around dawn and dusk. The gradual onset of the monsoon, with its early drizzles, nudges the heat wave to relax a little. The difference is more marked in Chandigarh, the common capital of Punjab and Haryana, due to its proximity to the Shivalik Range of the mighty Himalayas.

The evenings, especially around the eye-shaped Sukhna Lake at the foothills, are cooler than in other places in the vast plains of Punjab to the west and northwest of Chandigarh. The monsoon breeze touches the surface of the lake like a feather, sending gentle ripples through the water. It then seems to romance the tall gulmohars, oaks, peepals, eucalyptuses and mango trees—which sway in ecstasy—before gently caressing their leaves. These trees rise along the two-and-a-half km curved promenade of the lake.

Such weather would usually make people button up their long-sleeve shirts.

The lake came up by damming the rain-fed Sukhna rivulet in 1958, when Chandigarh was built as the first planned city of independent India. French architect Le Corbusier and Chief Engineer L. Verma designed the lake to attract humans, birds and aquatic species.

Over the years, Sukhna Lake became home to several species of birds, besides serving as a temporary abode for migratory avians from far-off Siberia as well. The atmosphere has remained serene despite the presence of a couple of hundreds of locals, besides tourists from various parts of India and abroad.

In such a romantic setting, one always finds lovers, newlyweds, and young and elderly couples, talking in hushed whispers. The birds, on the other hand, create a cacophony now and then, out of the sheer excitement and merriment of their own world. The music of their calls is never noise to the ears. It doesn't disturb the tranquillity of the place. In fact, humans are barred from making noise lest they disturb the ecology, particularly the birds and the aquatic life. One enters a capsule of silence at the site, where one is more in communion with oneself. Even those indulging in paddle boating in the lake do so in silence

On 6 July 2006, gunshots shattered such a poetic evening at the lake. Birds who had settled well in their homes on the trees, flapped about their wings in panic, screeching loudly.

The shots were fired near the Sukhna Lake Club (Lake Sports Complex today), a hangout for the elite of the city, who enjoy drinks and dinner sitting on the lush lawns, if not inside. The club extends from the lake on one side to the Kansal green belt and the famous Nek Chand Saini's Rock Garden on the other.

That evening, there were no visible signs of rain. Unknown at that time, sinister clouds were hovering above. These would not bring rain; instead, these would raise the temperature of the state again, setting off a chain of events that continue to this day.

Two killers were on the prowl, waiting behind one of the

bushes separating the club from the lake. And they kept watch on a Sikh youth, easily identifiable by his trademark *teddi pugri* (tilted turban) and large vulture-like eyes, dining on the lawns of the Lake Club with his friends, some of whom belonged to Punjab's powerful echelons. He was Prabhjinder Singh Brar, popularly known as Dimpy Chandbhan, and acknowledged by the police, media and in the criminal records as the first gangster of Punjab, or even that part of North India comprising Punjab, Haryana, and Himachal Pradesh besides Jammu and Kashmir.

Around 8.15 p.m. that day, the tall, lanky Dimpy walked out of the club unarmed with his cousin Navbir Singh alias Baboo, towards a blue Maruti Swift parked across the road, with the residence of the Chief Minister of Punjab at one end and that of the Governor of Haryana at the other. This road also had branches leading to the Punjab and Haryana High Court, Punjab Civil Secretariat, and Vidhan Sabha, besides the Rock Garden.

It is not unusual to see traffic cops or patrol vehicles on this VVIP road, or even a police *nakka* (checkpost) on the lookout for drunken driving or miscreants.

That day, there was none.

Dimpy was wearing his usual white-shirt over khaki trousers. His flowing beard, longer at the centre and reaching beyond his chest, swayed a little in the gentle breeze. His large eyes, the most prominent facial feature, that intimidated the onlooker with just a stare, shone in the dark. 'Chandbhan would usually wear the Muktsari white kurta pyjama. But in Chandigarh, he would be in formals. However, he loved loose fitting clothes,' recalls Kiranbir Singh Kang, a senior Akali leader, who was also close to Dimpy's family through common friends.

Dimpy Chandbhan was Numero Uno, the first in a long list of Punjab gangsters that followed. The foremost to emerge as the Punjab 'gangster' in the mid-1990s, he set up an organized network of criminals, who had link-ups with notorious gangsters sheltered by politicians in Punjab, Haryana, Uttar Pradesh, Bihar, and South India.

Dimpy's cousin Navbir, who always addressed the gangster as his *Bhaaji* (elder brother), had accompanied him to the club. He was the prime witness to the events that unfolded that evening.

◆

'I need to step out and meet someone,' Dimpy had told his cousin in the Lake Club. Dimpy was dining in the club with about eight to ten close friends, including some high-profile friends like Vishvapreet Singh Cheema, former Officer on Special Duty (OSD) to the then Chief Minister of Punjab, Capt. Amarinder Singh. Also, in attendance was Gurmeet Singh Bawa, considered a right-hand man and close aide of Dimpy's.

The dinner was specially planned by a friend Aman Chopra and his brother Vijay Chopra in honour of the don. There was talk of Dimpy contesting the Punjab Assembly elections likely to be held in ten months' time in early 2007. The mood was charged. Easy banter flowed amidst loud cackles, clanking of whiskey tumblers and the occasional breaking of tandoori chicken bones.

A girl called up Dimpy a few times. 'Come out in the parking for a few minutes. I'm waiting,' she requested him over the phone. On Navbir's insistence, Dimpy shared that it was his girlfriend, Harneev, who was outside and wanted to meet him briefly.

Later, Navbir would tell the police that he had accompanied Dimpy outside the club right up to the road after crossing the club parking, to ensure Dimpy's safety.

They passed Dimpy's Hyundai i20 in the parking without noticing the flat tyres.

Navbir spotted a blue Maruti Swift with the registration number CH 03S 4083 grinding to a halt near the Sukhna Lake Bus Stop shelter. He recognized the vehicle and the girl immediately. He had seen both earlier. She was Harneev alias Honey, Dimpy's girlfriend. Navbir later told the police that he had advised Dimpy to stay away from Harneev, a married woman with a son.

He saw Dimpy walking gently towards the car.

Of medium height, Harneev had a peculiar pair of eyes—sad and full of life at the same time—on her round cherubic face. She was on the driver's seat, and in her right hand dangled a cell phone from which she had exchanged several calls and messages with the gangster.

Navbir told the police that he had stopped there, and headed back to the club. But hardly had he taken a few steps when he heard ear-splitting gunshots.

◆

Punjab—Land of Five Rivers ('Punj' means five; 'ab' means water)—in 2006 was neither so used to such shootings, nor was it totally immune to them.

The state had achieved over a decade of peace after 15 long years of terrorism and insurgency, following the call to establish Khalistan—the pure land—a country for the Sikhs, independent from India. An estimated 50,000 people including cops, terrorists and civilians died during this dark period.

It all started with a clash between two Sikh organizations—the Akhand Kirtani Jatha and the Damdami Taksal that took on the Nirankari Mission on 13 April 1978 to propagate a human being as a living guru. Sikhism prohibits worshipping a human being as God. For Sikhs, the *Guru Granth Sahib*, compiled by Sikh Gurus and saints, and containing *bani*s of the ten Sikh Gurus, is the living Guru. The insurgency, fully supported by Pakistan, began in all earnest in April 1980 when Ranjit Singh, a firebrand Akali leader, shot dead Gurbachan Singh, Head of the Nirankari Mission.

The Khalistan movement reached a turning point with Operation Blue Star, mounted by the Indian Army on the Golden Temple in Amritsar—the most revered Sikh Gurdwara—and the Akal Takht—the temporal seat of the Sikhs. The storming of the Golden Temple led to the assassination of Indira Gandhi, the then Prime Minister of India, on 31 October 1984, by her two Sikh bodyguards, and the subsequent anti-Sikh riots across the country. Besides Prime Minister Indira Gandhi, the then Chief of Army Staff General A.S. Vaidya was shot dead by four assassins of the Khalistan Commando Force on 10 August 1986 as retribution for carrying out Operation Blue Star. Barely a year earlier, on 20 August 1985, Harchand Singh Longowal, the then president of the Shiromani Akali Dal, was killed just months after he had signed the Punjab Peace Accord with the then Prime Minister Rajiv Gandhi.

The Chief Minister of Punjab Beant Singh was killed on 31 August 1995, closer to the tail end of the insurgency. Not many untoward incidents happened after that.

The end of terrorism saw the revival of trade. Markets remained open till late. Marriage parties were held again. During the years of terrorism, *kharku*s—militants who fight for a cause and resent being called terrorists—had laid down strict rules against lavish marriage parties. The number of attendees could not cross eleven at best. No dowry or pompous display of power or position was allowed. Liquor vends remained open only during the day. In fact, many preferred to stay away from the business altogether.

Unfortunately, the revival of trade was marked by a surge in illegal practices too. The liquor trade is such that prices of a given brand and quantity of whisky, rum or wine can differ from district to district and from state to state. Each liquor vend has a designated area in which the seller is permitted to supply to marriage palaces,[1] parties, hotels, and bars. This encouraged the smuggling of liquor from one district or state to another to make a fast buck. To smuggle liquor to other districts or states, and to prevent other traders from selling liquor in one's notified area, musclemen were required. Musclemen were in demand in politics as well. They assured crowd at rallies and voters at polling booths.

This is where men like Dimpy Chandbhan came in handy. He had links with student leaders, businessmen, cops and powerful politicians not just in Punjab but also in the neighbouring state of Haryana and even Uttar Pradesh.

And he had an impressive criminal record that fit the bill.

◆

Dimpy Chandbhan's rise began in 1983 on the campus of Panjab University—a more than 100 years old educational institution

---

[1]In Punjab (and much of North India), a 'marriage palace' is a large, purpose-built venue for weddings and other major social functions. It is not a palace in the literal sense; the term refers to a banquet-hall complex, usually spread over several acres and designed to host lavish events.

which was just into the fourth year of holding student elections. The university was first established in Lahore (now Pakistan) in 1882. After Partition, the university opened on 1 October 1947 in Solan. During 1958–60, it moved to Sector 14, Chandigarh but the student elections could be held only in 1977, immediately after the end of the infamous Emergency.

From 1977 to 1980, the elections were largely trouble-free, barring some tense moments. By 1981–82, Parminder Cheema, who backed the Progressive Students Union (PSU), and Makhan Singh, president of the Punjab University Students Union (PUSU), had emerged as the principal rivals.

Jaskaran Brar, founder general secretary of PUSU, recalls Makhan as a burly Jat from Karnal, Haryana. About 5'10" tall and heavily built, Makhan was a law student who, according to his batchmates, was always eager for a fight. Though a couple of inches short of six feet, he carried a commanding presence.

'You could see most youngsters wearing their heart on their sleeves, all ready to jump into the lake of love and even be consumed by it. But Makhan wore his attitude on his rolled-up sleeves, ready to deliver a fist anytime,' recalls his compatriot Jaskaran Brar. Makhan's aura was intimidating.

Cheema was the son of a DSP (District Superintendant of Police) with the Punjab Police and often carried a pistol. He boasted of his connections and unabashedly brandished the pistol that he carried in contravention of all campus regulations.

Terrorism had already taken root in Punjab, and the police had just started getting unbridled powers. The Panjab University campus was yet to be fully disturbed by groups supporting the Khalistan movement, or directly helping the terrorists. The student groups had no direct affiliation with political parties but surely they had the 'blessings' of certain parties or key leaders—including a sitting Chief Minister of

Punjab and another who would later become President of India. *The Tribune* and *The Indian Express* often carried stories on student elections on the front page.

At that time, Dimpy Chandbhan was nowhere on the scene.

None among the warring groups could be classified as criminal. But the disturbing signs were visible. For these groups, it was all about an assessment of their respect among the students. Those who followed their diktat and submitted to their authority were supporters, and those expressing even a minor disagreement or not showing proper respect were perceived as enemies. A minor slight became a matter of life and death. The culture of moving around in groups, treating the university as their personal fiefdom, proving their one-upmanship—all was on full display. Unfortunately, that culture continues to this day.

Makhan Singh was one dominating figure among student leaders. These were the youths often referred to as *mooch-kaddu gabru*—one who twirls his moustache—and for whom, every issue was a *mooch da swaal*—a matter of self-esteem. 'It is a show of one-upmanship,' says Prof. Manjit Singh, a political scientist. 'The feudal mentality of dominating others with the power of muscles and weapons is exhibited by such groups. Sadly, even among senior politicians, this is continuing. You often see Punjab politicians daring each other openly for a fight, or that "I will smash your ego," so frequently used in election rallies, press statements, and even in discourses at the Punjab Assembly.'

The September 1983 elections are still remembered as the most fiercely contested ones. Earlier that year, Makhan had completed his degree in Law, and soon became a practising lawyer in Karnal.

The PUSU group faced immense trouble during campaigning. With the powerful Makhan Singh out of the way, the other groups dominated the election campaign to such an extent that the PUSU candidates could not even put up posters. Rajinder Deepa, a candidate for the president post from PUSU, and his supporters decided to paste campaign posters on the walls at midnight. But the other group got wind of it. By dawn, the opponents had already torn down the PUSU candidates' posters.

Undaunted, the PUSU members thought of re-pasting the posters around 6 a.m. But they were busted the next day. Armed supporters of the Cheema group then raided Rajinder's hostel. Many carried weapons. One of them was wearing a long kurta over a *chadra* (lungi or a wrap-around for men). That youth was Sandeep Bhau, who would run his own legacy of crime and gangsters for several decades in Punjab. Rajinder and the other candidates then called up Makhan Singh in Karnal, seeking his return to the campus.

The return of Makhan Singh turned the tables, and electioneering for PUSU picked up as did the fear of violence. And to counter Makhan, the rivals too called someone for help.

On polling day, heavy police force was deployed on the campus. SSP (Senior Superintendent of Police) Chandigarh G.S. Aujla had made elaborate arrangements. An officer of the Border Security Force (BSF), he was on deputation with the Punjab government. Despite the police bandobast, word soon spread that several outsiders had managed to slip in. Rajinder recalls specific intelligence about two motorcyclists from the Cheema group, who were believed to be capable of harming PUSU supporters in order to influence the voting.

Makhan Singh and the others were on the alert and standing near the Law Bhawan when the motorcyclists drove close to them. In a jiffy, Makhan caught hold of the pillion rider and pulled him down. But before he and the others could question them, the pillion rider pointed a gun at him.

That was none other than Dimpy Chandbhan—a name that would gain notoriety later on.

For a while, there was stunned silence as the pillion rider, Dimpy, pointed a gun at Makhan Singh. But before he could do anything else, an ardent supporter of Makhan from Tohana, fondly called Kaptaan Sahib, emerged from the bushes and lunged at Dimpy. Makhan seized the opportunity and snatched the gun. In the process, the gun went off, and hit Togatia, one of the PUSU candidates who was at a distance on his motorcycle. The bullet pierced his abdomen. He fell down, and suffered injuries on his legs as well when the motorcycle also fell on him.

An angry Makhan pounced on Dimpy, who was badly beaten. Others including Jaskaran Brar also joined on. Jaskaran grabbed Dimpy by his long hair. Dimpy suffered several fractures including on his face besides sustaining a bullet injury in his hand. Later, students supporting Dimpy's group arrived on the scene and took him to hospital.

Dimpy is said to never have forgotten that beating at the hands of Makhan Singh. 'He was not a student of Panjab University. He had no business to be here. It was a one-to-one fight and Makhan Singh proved too strong for him,' recalls one of the old leaders.

◆

Conflict in Panjab University

The PUSU, led by Rajinder Deepa, swept the elections. A news report in *The Tribune* dated 5 September 1983 termed the poll results as a defeat for the Darbara Singh group of the Congress party. Darbara Singh was the Chief Minister of Punjab at the time.

Darbara Singh's greatest political rival was none other than his own party colleague Giani Zail Singh, the then Union Home Minister. Later, Giani Zail Singh became President of India, and enjoyed closer access to Prime Minister Indira Gandhi. The rivalry between Darbara Singh and Giani Zail Singh has often been seen as one of the factors influencing terrorism in Punjab. Writers like B.D. Pande, former Governor of Punjab, journalist Jagtar Singh and many others have often discussed how the two misused the police, the central government and Punjab's religious leaders in their bid to checkmate each other.

Giani Zail Singh supported Rajinder Deepa's group. *The Tribune* described the election result through a glaring heading: Pro-Darbara group routed in varsity poll.

It detailed: 'The Progressive Students Union (PSU) patronised by certain Congress (Indira) men supporting the Punjab Chief Minister Darbara Singh was routed today in the annual election to fill four key posts in the Panjab University Students Council.'

Next day, *The Tribune* reported that Punjab Government had recalled SSP Chandigarh G.S. Aujla: 'The decision of the state government came within a few hours of the Progressive Students Union's stunning defeat in the Panjab University poll here yesterday.' It was mentioned in a later paragraph that: 'On the other hand, the Panjab University Students Union (PUSU) which enjoys the support of the Giani Zail Singh faction of the Congress won all the seats with a thumping majority.'

The news items show how bigwig politicians took not only an interest in the Panjab University students' elections but also tried to influence these. The elections became a nursery for future leaders and sadly, gangsters too. Every gangster worth his salt in Punjab owes his genesis directly or indirectly to these elections.

The 1983 election rivalry between these groups had been personal for the leaders long ago. The polling day incident of the gunshot injury to leader Togatia and the beating of an outsider, Dimpy Chandbhan, made the men blood-thirsty.

◆

The police investigation into the election violence revealed that Dimpy was not a student of Panjab University. His family hailed from Chandbhan village near Kotkapura in Faridkot District. Dimpy's grandfather, Gurbachan Singh, had once owned nearly 150 acres of land spread across Chandbhan village, Nabha town in Patiala District, and Bhawanigarh in Sangrur.

A close relative, Khushwinder Singh—whose aunt was married to Dimpy's father—said the family were big landlords. 'Some chunks of the land were sold off or donated to a religious place,' he said. 'Gurbachan had two sons and calculating the division of the property, Dimpy owned about 60 acres of land.

'Gurbachan's son Amarjit Singh, Dimpy's father, chose to live in Chandbhan village, while his brother Joginder Singh moved to Nabha town. Amarjit was the first person in the village to get an electricity connection—a distinction that would prove fatal. He died after being electrocuted in an agricultural field.'

It is not uncommon for farmers, big or small, in Punjab to climb transformer junctions to repair a short circuit. At the time of his father's death, Dimpy was studying in Class VIII at St Joseph's Convent School in Bathinda. For the higher secondary classes, he was enrolled at Shivalik School,

Mohali. Later, he was admitted in Government Rajindra College, Bathinda, where he got in touch with two students who wielded power. One was Honey, the son of a SSP, and another Sandeep Bhau, a student leader.

Khushwinder says: 'Dimpy first tasted power in their company and never looked back. Clashes with rival students become common and he suddenly seemed to have become a man who only listened to himself.'

Dimpy later joined Government College for Men in Sector 11, Chandigarh. It was here that he got in touch with members of the Cheema group and became involved in Panjab University election politics. 'I was his trusted relative. He would always call me whenever he was in trouble. But the problem was that he did not listen to any advice and just loved occupying centre stage, surrounded by followers,' recalls Khushwinder, who, later, also spent some years in jail as he was charged as co-conspirator with Dimpy in some cases.

One of the first major cases was about the kidnapping of a woman. Dimpy was in Class XI in Government Rajindra College, Bathinda, at the time. He and his friends had grown close to a political leader—now deceased—who often lent them his car to show off on campus. Though married, the leader had fallen in love with his wife's sister.

Khushwinder continues, 'The leader wanted Dimpy and his group of friends, or hooligans as I called them, to help kidnap the woman he was in love with.' During the kidnapping bid, gunshots were exchanged and the leader got injured. Dimpy and his friend were booked for kidnapping. I was also booked as a co-conspirator. I was the one who was his guardian in the college.'

Khushwinder insists Dimpy's widowed mother had brought him up as a pampered boy, who enjoyed many luxuries and always had his way. He would get anything he desired, but there was more he craved. He wanted respect, authority and followers—desires that would see many landlords in Punjab become students' leaders and then turn gangsters in Chandigarh—the battlefield for fiefdom. And revenge was a must. For Dimpy, the beating at the hands of Makhan Singh hurt the most.

◆

On 24 March 1985, Makhan, who had resumed his practice as an advocate in Karnal, arrived in Chandigarh to attend a court hearing regarding the violence during elections on the campus. In the evening, he was sitting in a service lane next to a rented house in Sector 16 and enjoying drinks with three friends. This was a routine for Makhan Singh whenever he visited Chandigarh. He would sit in the service lane and keep an eye on the road to spot any prospective killer. He was a heavy drinker. Not satisfied with the quantity he'd had, he sent one of the peg-mates to fetch more liquor. But the man was taking too long. The restless Makhan kept getting up to check the street to see if he was coming back.

Unknown to him, two men had entered his house scaling the wall from the back lane. They carried a 9mm and a Sten gun. They opened fire when Makhan was standing, craning his neck to see his friend. Makhan had a pistol tucked into his trouser but could not get it out in time to fire. As he fell, the killers came nearer and pumped several rounds into him.

He took 28 bullets, several from point-blank range when the killers came close to him. Yet, Makhan died some 40 minutes later, hurling abuses and swearing revenge.

The Tribune dated 25 March 1985 carried the news as the lead story on the first page, reporting twin killings in Chandigarh. The second was the death of Krishan Lal Manchanda, a BJP leader, who was killed in Sector 19. According to subsequent news reports, Manchanda's killing was carried out by terrorists but the police never said Makhan's killing was related to terrorism in Punjab.

One of Makhan's friends, who was 'enjoying' drinks with him on the day of the murder, received a letter threatening him with dire consequences if he dared identify the assailants. *The Tribune* dated 21 April detailed this letter and mentioned no one was identified.

It was only on 7 May that the police announced the suspects in the Makhan Singh murder case. According to a report in *The Tribune* on 8 May, during a briefing on the arrest of eight terrorists, some allegedly responsible for the killing of the BJP leader Manchanda, police officials said the prime suspects in the Makhan Singh murder case were Dimpy Chandbhan and Sandeep Bhau, but both were absconding. Also absconding were some other student leaders of Panjab University, who went abroad after hatching the conspiracy.

On 23 May, the Chandigarh Police announced that Gurinder Singh alias Satinder Singh, one of Makhan Singh's killers, had been arrested after a brief encounter. Gurinder is said to have met Khalistani leader Sant Jarnail Singh Bhindranwale. He too was close to a Congress minister, whose son also became a minister in various Congress-led governments. Gurinder succumbed to his injuries two days later. On 29 July, the police announced the arrest of Prabhjinder Singh alias Dimpy Chandbhan, and said he was nabbed a few days ago.

'He was arrested from Faridkot in the kidnapping case of a woman, which was still pending against him. He was later arrested in the Makhan Singh case,' said Khushwinder, his relative and guardian.

The news reports also said another suspected assailant Rajinder Mann was arrested from Amrawati, Maharashtra, where he had fled to after Makhan Singh's murder. The news report named Parminder Singh Cheema as the conspirator who had fled to New Zealand. Rajinder Mann already carried a bounty of ₹5,000 for looting a petrol pump in Sector 15, Chandigarh.

The police also announced a ₹1 lakh reward for any information on Sandeep Bhau whose whereabouts were unknown.

Sandeep was the one who had carried a Sten gun in the Panjab University campus and threatened Rajinder Deepa earlier. Sandeep was a youth leader from Bathinda, where his family owned more than 100 acres of land. He too used to throw his weight around in student politics.

Sandeep fled from Punjab, and is believed to have crossed over to Pakistan. In the absence of a border fence between the two countries, crossing over from one country to another was no big deal. The Pakistan security forces behind the Inter-Services Intelligence (ISI) and several Khalistani organizations welcomed such people, hoping to use them in the separatist movement. Later, Sandeep would face charges under the Terrorist and Disruptive Activities (Prevention) Act (TADA). From Pakistan, he moved to New Zealand and remained there for a while.

None of these people were convicted in the case. In fact, no one was ever convicted for the killing of Makhan Singh. But the months Dimpy spent in jail brought him close to terrorists and hardened criminals, some of whom had links with gangsters in other parts of the world. By then, he had already become a big name at Panjab University as he had brought down Makhan Singh.

It was probably this time in jail when Dimpy first heard about Mukhtar Ansari, the don of Uttar Pradesh. Out on bail, Dimpy was often spotted with Simranjit Singh Mann, an IPS officer-turned-Khalistani ideologue. Mann, a distant relative of Dimpy's, was at the time spearheading the Khalistan movement and contesting elections through his party, the Shiromani Akali Dal (Amritsar).

Dimpy first planned to contest elections from Kotkapura (Faridkot) in 1989, and again in 1991, but on both occasions the elections were postponed. Mann projected him as the candidate of his party Shiromani Akali Dal (Amritsar) for the Kotkapura Assembly elections.

The Mann group won six seats in the 1989 Lok Sabha elections, with three independents also winning with their support. Dimpy is seen in photographs with Mann besides several other political leaders. A number of Shiromani Akali Dal leaders of the Parkash Singh Badal faction, besides the Gurcharan Singh Tohra faction, also remained in the good books of Dimpy. The scheduled Assembly elections were not held due to the imposition of President's Rule.

It was in the mid-1990s that Dimpy met Mukhtar Ansari for the first time. The Uttar Pradesh don was in hiding in Haryana as the first BJP-led government under Kalyan Singh had assumed power in UP. A youth named 'Hitler' who used to study in Panjab University was part of Dimpy's inner circle. Hitler's family had political links and provided shelter to the fugitive don.

Mukhtar Ansari belonged to an illustrious family, whose members included one of the founders of Jamia Millia Islamia University, a Sufi saint, and even a Maha Vir Chakra winner. His grandfather Dr Mukhtar Ahmed Ansari was a surgeon educated in England, who earned popularity for grafting animal testicles onto humans. He was once President of the Indian National Congress during India's freedom struggle. Mukhtar's maternal grandfather Brigadier Mohammad Usman was awarded the Maha Vir Chakra during the Indo-Pakistan War in 1947. Hamid Ansari, an elder cousin of Mukhtar, was Vice-President of India for a decade—from 2007 to 2017.

Ansari faced around 60 criminal cases, including several for murder. He was booked for his first murder in 1986—a year after Dimpy was booked for his first murder, even though Ansari had already been booked for a brawl in 1978. Like Dimpy, he remained active in student elections.

Mukhtar could only be convicted in 2022, when the BJP-led NDA government was at the centre and the party's government was in power at Uttar Pradesh. He was found guilty in the murder case of BJP MLA Krishnanand Rai, who was killed in 2005 while he was on his way home after inaugurating a cricket tournament.

As the Congress was losing its sheen across India, Mukhtar took refuge in Punjab where the Congress government ruled under Capt. Amarinder Singh. Mukhtar was on the run from the BJP-led government in Uttar Pradesh, that had ordered a crackdown on gangsters, and the police did not shy away from encounters. For almost two years, the Punjab government refused to allow the transit remand of Mukhtar Ansari back to Uttar Pradesh. Eventually, he was shifted to Banda Jail in Uttar Pradesh in April 2021, where he died of a heart attack on 28 March 2024.

◆

Mukhtar was on the lookout for daring youngsters, and the fatherless Dimpy needed a godfather.

The connection with Mukhtar Ansari gave Dimpy access to a national network of gangsters. Soon, he was firmly on the path to becoming one of Punjab's most feared figures. Their relationship forged a powerful syndicate linking gangsters from Punjab and Uttar Pradesh, a network that went on to carry out multiple kidnappings. Like Mukhtar, Dimpy would later begin scouting for young talent of his own, sowing the seeds of gangsterism across Punjab.

In 1992, the Beant Singh-led Congress government won the Punjab Assembly elections, with the rival Shiromani Akali Dal (Amritsar) boycotting the polls. With no one identified or convicted in the Makhan Singh murder case, Dimpy was a free man. More importantly, he was now under Mukhtar's tutelage. By then, Mukhtar had entered politics as a Congress leader, which meant Dimpy also enjoyed a degree of protection from the Congress-led establishment at the Centre.

With the Beant Singh government in power, a massive crackdown on terrorism followed across Punjab. Criminals and gangsters, including Dimpy, fled the state. Once again, Mukhtar Ansari provided him shelter and protection.

This period also saw the rise of several *bahubali*s (super strong men) and gangsters in Uttar Pradesh—among them Brijesh Mishra and Dhananjay Singh—who began challenging Mukhtar's dominance. Extortion was no longer a cakewalk. Even so, Dimpy remained active in student politics at Panjab University, quietly scanning the campus for fresh recruits.

One such follower was Jaswinder Singh, alias Rocky Fazilka, from Fazilka. A wealthy landlord with nearly 40 acres of land, Rocky craved the respect and following that Dimpy commanded. Dimpy kept him close. Rocky was fond of weapons, and Dimpy would often hand him his own gun to carry—like indulging a child with a favourite toy. It was also a measure of the trust Dimpy placed in him.

Dimpy got married in 1996. The wedding became a public display of power.

Karanbir Singh, an Akali leader whom Dimpy treated like an elder brother, recalled that several high-profile politicians attended the ceremony, which was dominated by men brandishing weapons. 'It was madness,' he said. 'There were guns everywhere. No need for firecrackers—people just fired shots into the air. Mukhtar Ansari was there, along with many of his men. At one point, high on celebration, they lined up and fired hundreds of rounds at tall eucalyptus trees until the trunks collapsed.'

Kang, Dimpy's senior in school, said he had tried repeatedly to pull him back from the slippery slope. 'I even slapped him once in anger,' Kang recalled, 'but he was on a high, with the power of guns and dons and politicians at his feet.'

By then, Dimpy had already begun orchestrating kidnappings—crimes that would later surface in police records. In 1995, Dimpy and his gang carried out the sensational kidnapping of Subash Aggarwal, a businessman from Baddi, an industrial town near Chandigarh. Rocky was among his accomplices. News reports said the gang pocketed a ransom of ₹1.3 crore. Another businessman, Nand Kishore Rungta of Varanasi, was similarly abducted. A ransom of ₹1.25 crore was extracted, but Rungta was not released; he was killed. It was only in 2023—26 years later—that Mukhtar Ansari was finally jailed for this crime.

From Varanasi, Mukhtar's gang moved operations to South India. Their next target was Nirmal Singh Jaipuria, a diamond merchant known for his early morning walks with his dog, Boxy. On 15 July 1997, at around 5.50 a.m., Jaipuria stepped out for his routine walk. At about 6.45 a.m., the dog returned home bleeding. That was when the family realized something had gone terribly wrong.

Dimpy, the gang leader, was the first to be arrested — caught while making ransom calls from a public call office (PCO). His accomplices, including Jaswinder Singh Rocky, were arrested soon after, once Dimpy revealed their hideouts.

A Karnataka court later acquitted Dimpy and the others of kidnapping charges but convicted them for illegal possession of arms. The state appealed, but in November 2003, the Supreme Court acquitted all the accused, holding that the prosecution had failed to prove the kidnapping. The victim had not identified them as his abductors. There were reports that a Dubai-based don had pressured the businessman into turning hostile.

In March 2000, while serving a sentence, Dimpy escaped from custody—an episode that appeared anything but accidental. The Haryana Police had taken him on remand from Karnataka for questioning in a weapons-supply case. He escaped during transit. Investigators suspected that his political connections—Mukhtar Ansari, senior Congress leaders and influential Akali figures in Punjab—had helped engineer the breakout.

Dimpy remained underground until October 2002, when he was arrested by the Delhi Police. Punjab Police later secured his transit remand and lodged him in Bathinda Jail. He was accused of ordering the murder of a liquor contractor —a former partner who had 'dared' to operate liquor vends independently.

When Dimpy was released from Bathinda Jail in 2004, he was given a grand welcome. Supporters cutting across political parties and communities brought him home in a cavalcade of nearly 500 cars. It set a template that many gangsters continue to follow.

Ironically, such public adulation often marks the beginning of the end. Politicians queued up like ants around jaggery to be seen with Dimpy—until he became a liability, or worse, aligned with a rival camp. It is a pattern that has played out repeatedly in the arc of Punjab's gangsters.

◆

With such following and proximity to powerful figures, Dimpy had fearlessly walked out of the Lake Club on 6 July 2006 and hopped into the front seat of the car. He took out a gold chain from his pocket. Harneev's eyes lit up. She stretched out her hand to take it, extending her palm like a cup—when she heard a loud bang. Dimpy screamed as he collapsed beside her. Shards of glass flew around.

As bullets struck both occupants of the car, their terrified screams pierced the silence. Splinters hit Harneev on the right side of her face, shattering her jawbone and several teeth, while another bullet smashed the mobile phone dangling from her right hand, severing one of her fingers.

Somehow managing to accelerate the idling engine, Harneev sped away, taking a U-turn towards the Haryana Governor's residence, which further down led to her house in Sector 8. She chose that route because the motorcycle-borne shooters had fled in the opposite direction, towards the High Court end of the road.

Dimpy's head lay in her lap.

As she swerved past the Haryana Governor's residence, half of Dimpy's lifeless body slipped out through the door, which had flung open. She dragged him back inside and drove straight to her home, about a kilometre and a half away, screaming all the way.

Harneev's parents rushed them to the Government Multi-Speciality Hospital in Sector 16, but it was too late. At 9.20 p.m., Dimpy Chandbhan was declared brought dead.

The post-mortem found three bullets lodged in the abdominal region and two in the right shoulder. Seven empty cartridges were recovered from the crime scene. The assailants had used .45 Ithaca pistols.

Kiranbir Singh Kang was the one who received Dimpy's body from the hospital and performed ardas at his cremation.

'You have seen Sidhu Moosewala's cremation. The number of mourners at Dimpy's cremation was no less. He had direct access to many ministers, and even chief ministers of Punjab, Haryana and Uttar Pradesh. He never said no to anyone who sought his help in legal or illegal work. He had such charisma that anyone, even a senior cop, who spent a short time with him, would become his friend for life.'

Some 14 years later, Punjabi rap singer Sidhu Moosewala would make Dimpy's teddi pugri famous again, while mentioning Dimpy in his song 'Malwa Block', underscoring the 'dare' and raw courage of Punjab's first gangster. Moosewala compared himself to Dimpy, saying he too was 6 feet-plus like Dimpy, and also wore a teddi pugri.

Moosewala would not live long after singing that song. Nearly 16 years after Dimpy was gunned down, Moosewala would be murdered on 29 May 2022, by six shooters sent by Lawrence Bishnoi—the most dreaded gangster of Punjab. But that was to unfold years after 2006.

Harneev later recalled seeing two shooters—one arriving on a motorcycle from the front and another on foot. Navbir also told the police that he had seen two assailants speeding away on a motorcycle, though he could neither note the registration number nor identify them.

Neither Harneev nor Navbir could identify the killers.

Unknowingly, the murder set a pattern that would repeat itself—betrayals followed by revenge, seen from the killers' perspective. In turn, the betrayers would be betrayed, triggering an endless cycle. From one gang, several others would mushroom.

Dimpy was never convicted for the murder of Makhan Singh. No one was ever convicted for Dimpy's murder either.

The Chandigarh Police failed to unravel the conspiracy. Investigators began by recording statements of everyone who had been partying with Dimpy at the Lake Club that evening, but none could shed light on either the plot or the assailants.

Suspicion soon turned towards Harneev. Was she part of the conspiracy? Yet she had risked her own life—the shooters had fired indiscriminately at the car. Was it sheer providence that she survived?

'The gold chain was not a gift from Dimpy. It was my chain,' Harneev told the police in her statement. 'The lock had broken. He had taken it from me to get it repaired. I had called him that evening to get it back.'

Simranjit Singh Mann, president of the Shiromani Akali Dal (Amritsar), later told this writer that he had proposed a marriage between Dimpy and Harneev several years earlier, but her parents had refused. Harneev was subsequently married to a businessman and had a son from that marriage. She and Dimpy later reconnected and began seeing each other. Dimpy, too, was married at the time and had a son.

At the insistence of the police, Harneev underwent a brain-mapping test. She also agreed to a narco-analysis test but failed to appear for it despite several court summons.

The police then narrowed their focus to key members of the Dimpy Chandbhan gang—men seen as claimants to its leadership after his death. Chief among them was Rocky Fazilka, who had been part of the gang involved in the Bengaluru businessman's kidnapping.

Rocky was questioned as a suspect. Inspector Amanjot, who later took premature retirement, was with the Chandigarh Police Crime Branch at the time of Dimpy's murder and had visited the crime scene. The case itself, however, remained with Police Station No. 3 of the Union Territory Police.

Inspector Amanjot and his colleagues suspected Rocky from day one. They had inside information suggesting that relations between Rocky and Dimpy were strained for some time. Explaining his suspicion, Amanjot said Rocky believed Dimpy had sidelined him. 'Dimpy kept most of the proceeds from the crime—the kidnappings and the extortion. He also "plotted" only his own escape from police custody, while Rocky and the others remained behind bars.'

The UT Police questioned Rocky. He denied all involvement but agreed to both a brain-mapping and a narco test. Like Harneev, however, he ultimately underwent only the brain-mapping test. It yielded no leads.

◆

A month before the second anniversary of the murder, the Crime Branch finally got the go-ahead to investigate the case. Inspector S.S. Rana and Sub-Inspector Amanjot Singh arrested Rocky on 29 July 2008—two years and 23 days after Dimpy's murder. The Crime Branch claimed it had recovered the .45-bore Ithaca pistol from Rocky.

Inspector Amanjot had also been part of the first Chandigarh Police team to reach the crime scene near the

Sukhna Lake Club. Later, his team recovered a memory card from the broken mobile phone of Harneev from her car. The card contained several call recordings, including the last conversation between her and Dimpy. Inspector Amanjot was also the officer who later recovered the Ithaca pistol from Rocky.

However, the court ruled that the mere recovery of the pistol from Rocky did not establish that he was the killer or that he had played any role in the murder conspiracy. An FIR was lodged against him under the Arms Act, 1959, for possessing a firearm without a valid licence.

The Crime Branch then claimed that during questioning, Rocky had admitted to being part of the conspiracy to kill Dimpy Chandbhan. In his disclosure statement, Rocky said: 'I, along with Sunil Kumar, Surinder Singh Advocate and Ravinder Singh alias Bhura, all residents of Meerut (Uttar Pradesh), conspired to kill Chandbhan. We did this on the direction of Mukhtar Ansari.'

He later retracted the statement in court, alleging that he had been pressured into making the confession.

According to Rocky, Sunil Kumar and Ravinder Bhura had fired at Dimpy using the .45 pistol recovered from him. He claimed that Surinder Singh Advocate had supplied the weapon and kept cartridges at his rented house in Meerut.

Forensic examination confirmed that the bullets recovered from Dimpy's body and the crime scene had been fired from the same weapon.

About two weeks later, on 13 August, Sub-Inspector Charanjit Singh of the Crime Branch and Sub-Inspector Ram Phal of UT Police Station, Sector 11, visited Meerut to verify Rocky's claims. Their inquiry revealed that Ravinder Bhura had been in jail since 23 May 2006—nearly two months before Dimpy's murder—and was incarcerated on the day of the crime, as confirmed by jail records.

Ravinder, however, did not live long. Just two months later, on 16 October 2006, five armed assailants shot him dead inside the Meerut court premises while he was attending a hearing in another case. Despite wearing a bulletproof jacket—provided because of threats to his life—Ravinder suffered fatal gunshot wounds. He had been escorted by a posse of 17 armed policemen, all in bulletproof gear. Even so, the attackers managed to kill him.

◆

The police were never able to trace Sunil Kumar and Surinder Singh Advocate.

As for Mukhtar Ansari's whereabouts, investigators found that he had been lodged in Ghazipur Jail in Uttar Pradesh since 25 October 2005. The investigation did not conclusively state whether Mukhtar did or did not hatch the conspiracy from inside prison. After all, incarceration does not necessarily preclude planning a crime; at best, it ruled out his role as a shooter.

The Chandigarh Police eventually gave Mukhtar Ansari a clean chit and concluded in their investigation report that Rocky's disclosure statement was false. Inspector Amanjot maintained that the findings of his investigation were watertight, but the court did not accept them.

Dimpy's family met a fate similar to that of his victims. They kept knocking on the doors of justice—shuttling between police stations, courts and the media. At a press conference in Chandigarh, reported by *The Tribune* on 11 October 2006, Dimpy's wife Pawandeep Kaur demanded a CBI probe into his murder. She, along with her father

Hardeep Singh Kadian and Dimpy's mother Gurpreet Kaur, alleged that politicians—including prominent figures from both the Shiromani Akali Dal and the Congress—had hatched the conspiracy.

To this day, Dimpy Chandbhan's killers have not been brought to book. Several theories have floated over the years. One suggested the involvement of state-level politicians after Dimpy decided to contest elections from Kotkapura—a move believed to have had the potential to influence results across multiple seats.

At one point, Dimpy had even brought rival gangs from Uttar Pradesh to the negotiating table, persuading them to stop working at cross-purposes. The initiative briefly cooled gang wars, but suspicion soon replaced trust.

Rajinder, a shooter associated with the Dhananjay gang, had an AK-47 meant to be delivered to his boss. Dimpy reportedly kept the rifle with him for a period before handing it over to Mukhtar Ansari instead—an act that allegedly turned the Dhananjay gang against him.

Dimpy also carried out several kidnappings with Rocky Fazilka. Over time, accusations of unfair distribution of ransom money created rifts between Dimpy, Rocky and other associates.

There was also talk of a senior Shiromani Akali Dal leader having called Dimpy a few days before the murder, urging him to refrain from contesting the Kotkapura seat. According to the family, Dimpy's growing influence had begun to threaten established political interests.

The family repeatedly named Rocky Fazilka and Sandeep Bhau as suspects in the murder. Ironically, Sandeep had earlier been an accomplice of Dimpy in the Makhan Singh murder case.

In 2012, Rocky Fazilka contested elections as an independent candidate from Fazilka, with the tacit support of the Shiromani Akali Dal (Badal).

The family also suspected Harneev Kaur's involvement in the conspiracy. 'She was the one who called Dimpy and asked him to come out alone to her car. How come she survived the hail of bullets?'

Harneev—abandoned by everyone—shut herself away from a world alive with memories of her lover.

A close aide of Dimpy, who had comforted Harneev after his murder, became her only companion. 'She drowned herself in alcohol as she faced infamy from her family, the gangsters, the media,' he said. 'And the police too constantly questioned her.'

The man, who agreed to speak to this writer after much persuasion and on strict condition of anonymity, revealed that he and Harneev grew very close. 'We were together almost all the time. Drinking and stuff. At times, it was even 20–24 bottles of beer a day. She would drink and cry. She would wake up and cry some more.'

Harneev died in February 2014 due to excessive drinking, just days after the Punjab and Haryana High Court acquitted prime accused Rocky Fazilka of the charge of killing Dimpy Chandbhan.

'At times, I felt I was with a living corpse,' the man recalled. 'She would drink till she dropped unconscious. The moment she would wake up, she would hit the bottle again. The body could not take that any more. Her soul had left it long ago. She had died that very evening with Dimpy.'

Harneev died next to him, crying that the men who killed her lover were still alive.

But would they survive? And for how long?

2

Rocky Fazilka

DIMPY CHANDBHAN ALWAYS KEPT HIS protégé Jaswinder Singh alias Rocky Fazilka by his side. Rocky belonged to Jhuggian Kesar Singh village in Fazilka District. Together, they made a formidable pair. The partners in crime enjoyed unchallenged supremacy in Punjab's underworld that extended to the northern states, with a hotline to Uttar Pradesh gangster-turned-politician Mukhtar Ansari.

They shared the same burning ambition and similar childhood backgrounds, yet they were studies in contrast. Police officers and acquaintances who had known both often spoke of their sharply different personalities.

Rocky was nearly 25 years younger than Dimpy. Dimpy epitomized rugged courage and boldness, exuding raw strength and fearlessness, while Rocky embodied sophistication and charm.

With his inimitable gait and swag, Dimpy had a domineering presence. Rocky was the silent one, with the air of a suave aristocrat. Clean shaven, he wore formal shirts and trousers or well-tailored suits with heeled leather shoes, rounding that off with expensive spectacles or goggles. Despite being quiet, he was always observing and taking mental notes while assessing others. One reason for his reserve was practical: unlike the convent-educated Dimpy, Rocky could not speak English. Silence helped preserve an aura of mystery around him. In simple terms, Rocky was the civilized version of Dimpy.

Dimpy wore loose-fitted shirts and trousers, with his trademark teddi pugri. Often, he would just wear the popular Muktsari white kurta pyjama and sandals. Police officials who investigated their cases or could question them often remarked that if Dimpy was the muscle, Rocky was the brain.

'Though silent and playing second fiddle to Dimpy, Rocky's mind was always at work, scheming new things and nursing ambitions of his own,' recalled a retired UT Police officer, speaking on condition of anonymity.

Dimpy showed a special preference for Rocky, especially during his meeting with high-profile people or when visiting clubs. Rocky was easy-going, with a warm smile, and made friends easily with a firm handshake.

Dimpy was the guru, and Rocky the disciple. Rocky did not just look up to Dimpy, he worshipped him to such an extent that he wanted to be him.

And somewhere along the way, he wanted to replace Dimpy.

Perhaps, that was why Rocky maintained a distinct persona. Did he sense that the future would not belong to street fighters but to smooth-talking dons with networks across the underworld—and among police officers and politicians—even as they played both sides?

Ironically, both build their fiefdom around Panjab University students' politics and elections, and yet, neither of them was even a graduate. Rocky remained a matriculate (according to the election affidavit that he had filed in 2012 when he contested the Punjab Assembly elections) and Dimpy was higher secondary (10+2) pass. Rocky did take admission in a prominent school for the higher secondary certificate but did not complete it.

Both men lost their respective fathers early in life. Dimpy was about eight years old when his father was accidentally electrocuted and died. His widowed mother brought him up.

Rocky was the second of three siblings. They lived in Jhuggian village in Fazilka, a district in southwest Punjab sharing an international border with Pakistan, and the state boundary with Rajasthan. The family owned about 70 acres of land. The eldest in the family, a daughter named Rajinder Kaur, was born in 1972, followed by Rocky in 1973, and the youngest, Romi, came along the year after.

Rocky's *tayaji* (elder paternal uncle) had no child of his own. So he had unofficially adopted Rocky as his son, though Rocky continued to live with his parents. Both Rocky and Romi seemed to have a troubled childhood. They had fast become tall and muscular, and were involved in street brawls.

Around 1994, Rocky's brother Romi and their father, Jaswinder Singh, frequently got into arguments. During one such argument, Romi shot dead his father. On the basis of a complaint lodged by his mother, Romi was booked for murder and sent to jail to face trial.

The worried family decided to send Rocky to boarding school in Chandigarh. It was there that he first met Dimpy. But Rocky was not involved in any criminal activity immediately. He had grown up hearing tales of Dimpy's exploits. So, he too wanted to become big. But he wanted his name to be feared by people who did wrong or immoral things. Once, when some goons were harassing a close friend's sister, he beat them in the Fazilka bazar. However, those young goons were politically connected, so Rocky had to flee to Chandigarh under Dimpy's protection. Did he see his lost father in Dimpy? Only Rocky could have answered that question.

Rocky's sister Rajdeep Kaur reveals that Dimpy came in contact with the family through the relative of a neighbour, who was also studying in Chandigarh. 'We sent Rocky to Chandigarh for higher studies and better company. How were we to know that he would fall into even more dangerous company—even greater trouble,' she and their mother lamented.

By that time, Dimpy was heavily into extortion. But as the rival gangsters of Uttar Pradesh began to raise their heads, Mukhtar Ansari and Dimpy planned some major strikes. For that, Dimpy needed followers, and not all of them were required to be bold and daring. Dimpy already had a large number of supporters in Panjab University. Another favourite place to hang out was the hostel in Government College for Men, in Sector 11.

◆

Dimpy Chandbhan and Rocky Fazilka carried out extortions and kidnappings with the Uttar Pradesh gangster Mukhtar Ansari, who enjoyed the support of the Congress government leaders in Punjab and some top national leaders.

Even today, gangsters in Punjab enjoy political patronage. Such support often works at cross purposes with rival factions, leading to immense struggle over fiefdoms, electoral battles, and, simply speaking, sheer domination. A gangster enjoys unbridled power when his political masters form the government; the same gangster may well take a bullet when another party comes to power.

Often, differences crop up in a group of gangsters due to a change of political masters.

As mentioned earlier, Dimpy and Rocky kidnapped businessman Subash Aggarwal from Baddi in 1995, followed by the kidnapping of another businessman in Bihar, and later of Nirmal Kumar Jaipuria in Bangalore. It was this kidnapping that went awry. All were caught, and with that came to light the previous kidnappings and ransoms collected. So grateful was Jaipuria to be rescued by the police that he offered to replace all the old police cars with brand new Tata Sumos.

Dimpy was the first to be nabbed. Then the others were caught. They spent considerable time in Bangalore, Delhi, Lucknow, and later Punjab jails. Yet the gang kept growing and becoming stronger from jail itself. Dimpy's network expanded far and wide, with the active help of Mukhtar Ansari.

Dimpy controlled the liquor business in many parts of Malwa, especially in the southwestern districts and towns of Faridkot, Muktsar, Fazilka, Ferozepore, Abohar, Bathinda and Moga, and earned protection money.

Liquor business in Punjab is one of the most coveted trophies of all Punjab gangsters once they emerge as the top don. The southwestern area is the creamy layer of the pie. This region shares state borders with Haryana and Rajasthan. Also, some gangs bring in drugs like opium and poppy husk from Rajasthan (Government of India allows licensed cultivation here) to Punjab in exchange of liquor, which they sell locally or smuggle further down to sell at a higher premium to Gujarat, a dry state.

The southwestern region also shares a porous international border with Pakistan, and falls in the drugs transit route that begins from Afghanistan and continues up to the metros of India via Punjab.

Another curious scenario is that liquor rates vary from one district to another *within* the state itself. This leads to inter-district smuggling as well. Then, at an even more micro level, a liquor vend owner can sell liquor in its designated area only. This means the liquor can't be delivered outside the earmarked region. Even a minor violation can lead to major disputes. And to resolve these disputes, one needs muscle power besides links with cops and politicians. And since it is commonplace to resort to illegal practices, the use of black money in the trade and the muscle power of gangsters often come in handy. Also, since much of the sale-purchase happens on credit, betrayal of trust leads to bloody disputes. At the same time, be it a small liquor trader or a liquor baron, no one likes another trying to seize control of his region. In case that happens, he needs to use muscle power. But someone with stronger muscle power always aims to grab more areas of the business.

Almost all gangsters of Punjab were involved in the murder or attempt to murder of one liquor trader or another. Dimpy was booked by Bathinda Police on 19 February 2004 for the alleged killing of Darshan Kumar Bajakhana, a wine contractor. The FIR named a Delhi liquor contractor as his co-accused in the murder case, which shows the wide interest in the liquor business of the region. Later, Rocky too would be booked for threatening or attacking liquor contractors. He even forged a partnership with controversial liquor-contractor-cum-Shiromani-Akali-Dal-leader Shiv Lal Doda, who contested the 2012 Assembly polls from Abohar when Rocky contested as an independent from the neighbouring Fazilka. Both helped each other.

◆

Rocky and Dimpy had been hand in glove but fissures had already begun to appear. Police officials said there was ill-will brewing over the 'unfair' distribution of the extortion money and the regular income from the liquor business, or protection trade. It was around this time that Rocky appears to have started his own innings.

The Congress government led by Capt. Amarinder Singh was in power in Punjab (2002-07). Owing to his connections with the Congress, the writ of Mukhtar Ansari had to be taken seriously. Much later, Mukhtar would 'enjoy' two years in Ropar (Punjab) Jail—from 2019 to 2021—as an undertrial in an extortion case. At that time too, under Capt. Amarinder Singh and later under Charanjit Singh Channi, the Congress government was in power. Mukhtar stayed in Ropar Jail amidst the most egregious display and abuse of power.

Rocky was said to be upset with Dimpy for handing over most of the ransom money to Mukhtar Ansari. It was this inside information which led Chandigarh Police to question Rocky as the prime accused in the Dimpy murder case. Also, while Rocky and the others remained behind bars in the Jaipuria kidnapping case till they were acquitted, Dimpy quietly plotted and executed his escape from custody, causing much resentment.

One of the reasons for the differences between Dimpy and Rocky was that Dimpy worked under the influence of Mukhtar Ansari. Knowing that he would never enjoy that kind of proximity to Mukhtar, Rocky began veering towards Dhananjay Singh and others. In Punjab, he was already close to the Akalis, who had wrested power from the Congress in 2007 and would rule till 2017.

Rocky was 32 at that time. He never got married. Rumour had it that he had some casual flings and relationships but nothing serious. A politician close to him said that arrests and the jail experience probably killed certain desires in him.

Chandigarh Police could not extract much information from him though. It was only two years later, in 2008, that a team led by Inspector Satbir Singh and Sub-Inspector Amanjot Singh were able to arrest Rocky for possessing an illegal weapon. The police found a .45 bore Ithaca pistol during a search at his residence and at other hideouts. This was the pistol that was used in the killing of Dimpy Chandbhan. However, the police could not get Rocky to confess to the crime, nor could they get any witness to testify against him.

On 5 February 2014, the Punjab and Haryana high court acquitted Rocky Fazilka. Various newspapers gave the acquittal front-page coverage. *The Tribune* reported that the police had arrested Rocky with the pistol used in the crime. In the chargesheet, the police stated that the dispute over distribution of ransom money was the main motive behind the murder. The prosecution said that Dimpy had denied Rocky and others their 'due' share even though the 'boys' had done most of the risky work. The reports also mentioned Ravinder Bhura, a shooter who had left the Ansari gang over some dispute and joined his rivals. (It was the same Bhura who had given an AK-47 to Dimpy to supply to a rival of Mukhtar Ansari. Instead, Dimpy had given the weapon to Mukhtar Ansari.)

At the court hearing, Rocky wore a white T-shirt over a pair of jeans. The rimless specs settled well on his pointed nose. He could have been mistaken for Bollywood star Vinod Khanna that day and later from his photos that appeared in the newspapers. He was said to be soft and humble while making a statement to the media after his acquittal. 'I was framed. I was falsely implicated by some political leaders of Punjab in connivance with Chandigarh Police. I was in

Delhi at the time the police showed my arrest from Sector 11, Chandigarh. Inspector Amanjot Singh of the Crime Branch and Inspector Kuldeep made a false case to gain mileage.'

Like Makhan Singh's murder, Dimpy Chandbhan's murder officially and legally remains a mystery.

◆

When Rocky was arrested for Chandbhan's murder, he was first kept in Burail Jail in Chandigarh and later shifted to Ferozepore and other jails. The transfer of an undertrial from one jail to another usually happens for two reasons—either for an official reason or due to the influence of the undertrial.

The official reason is that an inmate should be kept in a jail closest to the court that is hearing his case to facilitate travelling the shortest distance possible while taking the criminal to court. This also reduces the risk of the criminal either fleeing or being freed from police custody by his fellow gangsters.

Inmates like Rocky used their influence, mainly political, or their connections with the police to get transferred to a jail nearer their house or to a jail of their choice. In order to help an influential criminal, it is not uncommon for the police to seek his remand for questioning in a case. He is then brought to the concerned police district, and later housed in a local jail.

When outside the jail, Rocky would look to recruit young student leaders to his group, providing them support in the form of men and muscle power, vehicles, political shelter, and even weapons and hiding places. When in jail, Rocky would look for fresh talent. In the criminal world, 'daring' works—and it helps if the recruit can tap into the gang's existing network.

Rocky is believed to have met the notorious arms smuggler Ranjit Singh Dhillon alias Dupla in Burail Jail, in late 2008. Rocky had been arrested in July that year. With Dimpy no longer around to call the shots, Rocky was the lead gangster but in order to truly become the don, he needed to have his own army of criminals.

Dupla fit in perfectly. He was a leading arms smuggler with several police cases against him. Rocky and Dupla formed a lifelong association. They worked together and were booked together for arms supply. Both were arrested in March 2015 in Faridkot for possession of illegal arms and ammunition, which Dupla had brought for Rocky.

In December 2011, Chandigarh Police arrested Dupla with three sophisticated weapons—a .30 bore carbine, a 9mm pistol, and a .30 bore Chinese pistol, along with 159 live cartridges. Dupla seemed to be in circulation despite being arrested many times.

In jail, Rocky also met Gurshaheed Singh alias Shera Khuban. Through Shera, he got in touch with Vicky Gounder, Jaipal Bhullar, Gurpreet Sekhon, and Happy Deora—the top names in the world of gangsters.

Later, when Rocky was in Ferozpore Jail, he met Jaipal Bhullar and his main associate Chander alias Chandu. Rocky influenced all of them and soon they were part of one big group. Jaipal was an expert in highway robbery and carjacking. All of them had looted gun houses, banks, money exchange firms, and extorted money from businessmen as well.

Jaipal had a special relationship with Shera Khuban and Vicky Gounder as all of them had been award-winning sportspersons at one time. But they all went astray or perhaps life forced them into a life of crime.

While the bloody gang war that catapulted the Punjab

gangsters to the stature of the Mumbai mafia had not yet started, it wasn't too far away either.

Rocky, who enjoyed supremacy over the group, managed the young and hot-blooded emerging gangsters. He was known to never snap ties with anyone even if there were quarrels, misunderstandings and alleged betrayals. He was already following in the footsteps of Dimpy, eyeing the life of a politician, so that he could have a string of gangsters and the administration in his hands. Life would be different from when he simply did Dimpy's bidding.

This was bound to create trouble for others. When a criminal tries to become 'clean', he has to make sacrifices. And most often, he sacrifices others.

Now, Rocky needed his young men to use these weapons. The opportunity came when he was shifted to Ferozepore Jail. Jaipal and Chandu were incarcerated there while facing trial in a highway robbery case.

On his release from Ferozepore Jail, Rocky was no longer the person accused of killing Dimpy; he was a seasoned gangster brimming with confidence. He had connections with Dhananjay Singh, who had become even more powerful than Mukhtar Ansari. Rocky had his own group of followers, much in the same way he himself had once followed Dimpy Chandbhan. These followers—often referred to as sidekicks—drew their power and influence from men like Rocky and Dimpy.

What remained were the all-important connections with Punjab politicians. That was the protection Dimpy enjoyed during the Congress rule. The Congress would not warm up to Rocky as Mukhtar Ansari was livid at Dimpy's murder. So Rocky turned to the Akalis. Later, the Shiromani Akali Dal leaders would be clicked with Rocky Fazilka many a time.

To become a politician, one needs to have a clean image. Rocky Fazilka returned home in 2009 and decided to do social service. He had money and influence and soon started organizing durbars like the kings of yore, or like the Sangat Darshan organized by Shiromani Akali Dal chief Parkash Singh Badal at that time. Rocky resolved disputes faster than the courts and enjoyed the support of some police officials as well.

'When Rocky was alive, boys stopped indulging in eve-teasing. He thrashed many of them. Thefts and snatchings were not heard of,' Rajinder Kaur boasted about the influence of his brother.

In 2011, massive floods inundated Fazilka and the surrounding areas. These floods were caused by the badly swollen Sutlej River, which originates in Himachal Pradesh, and enters Pakistan at Hussainiwala, Ferozepore. India has put up barrages near the border to divert water to Rajasthan via Faridkot, Fazilka and Bathinda. Under the Indus Water Treaty (1960), India can stop the flow of water from Sutlej to Pakistan. The river in Pakistan turns southeast and flows along the border with Punjab (India). Whenever the river is in spate, India opens the barrages to ease the pressure. Though additional water is welcome, Pakistan has strengthened the banks of the river only on its side. As a result, during the monsoon, the river's span can increase to several hundred metres. This becomes a favourite route for drug smugglers, who use large tyre tubes to swim across to India with consignments of narcotics and then return just as deftly to their base.

Rocky became a messiah for the flood-affected people. He would reach their houses with food, medicines and clothes. He provided shelter to many and earned a good name for that.

For the Assembly elections, Rocky sought a ticket from

the Shiromani Akali Dal (SAD). However, the SAD had entered into an alliance with the BJP, whose senior leader Surjit Kumar Jyani was a sitting MLA from Rocky's area. He was also a Minister of Forest, Wildlife and Labour in the SAD-BJP government led by Parkash Singh Badal. Under the alliance, the SAD fought in 94 seats while the BJP candidates fought in the remaining 23 seats in the 117-strong Punjab Assembly. The seat Rocky wanted was in the BJP's kitty, and as the party had won it in the last elections, there was no reason for the Akalis to give it to their candidate—Rocky Fazilka.

The gangster then contested the elections as an independent. However, the SAD continued to help him secretly. This led to ugly situations between the alliance partners. Eventually, weeks before the elections, Rocky was booked and arrested for attempt to murder of a BJP activist in the area. The Akalis came clean by sending Rocky to jail. Yet, such was the steadfastness of Rocky's relationship with the SAD that a few years down the line, his sister Rajdeep Kaur joined the Shiromani Akali Dal formally.

Rocky lost the elections to Jyani by 1,692 votes. Before returning to jail, he had led a vitriolic poll campaign. He had attacked Jyani and others by referring to them as garbage. In each rally, he would say that he was not contesting elections based on the promise of providing paved streets and sewage systems in towns and villages, but on the promise to cleanse the garbage that had accumulated in society.

After his election loss and subsequent release from jail, Rocky roared at a rally, 'Yes, we lost. But don't think you and I will wait for our time, when we are in power, to take revenge of this defeat. Because this time too, victory or defeat notwithstanding, we are already in power and we will always be.' He said this indirectly, referring to his political connection in the SAD-ruled SAD-BJP government in Punjab.

While the tacit support of the Akalis may have helped Rocky put up a strong fight, he also got support from Dhananjay Singh; the Uttar Pradesh-based gangster-turned-politician had especially campaigned for him, using his own money and muscle power.

Meanwhile, members of Rocky's gang including Chandu, Happy Deora, Rajeev Raja, Shera Khuban, Vicky Gounder, Jaipal Bhullar and later Gurpreet Sekhon had been active, carrying out kidnappings, robberies, car jackings, murders and extortions. However, soon fissures began developing among the members as some, including Shera and Gurpreet, were helping Congress candidates in the Ferozepore region while Fazilka was helping Akali candidates. Jaipal and others were active around 2006 but none had the organizational skill of Fazilka, who had picked it up from Dimpy Chandbhan and later, from Dhananjay Singh.

Political rivalry created differences among the group members as well. At the same time, gangsters like Vicky and Shera were against Rocky's decision to contest elections. Later, this difference would become public.

Rocky indulged in extortion and took protection money from liquor vendors, sand contractors, and transporters, among others. In the gang was a youth named Happy Deora, who had grown closer to Rocky than the others. Happy along with Shera and others committed several robberies. On one such occasion, they looted a gun depot in Hoshiarpur. In the biggest crime of its kind in the state, as many as eight guns of different models were stolen. Punjab Police and even central security agencies were desperate to track down the robbers.

The first to be nabbed by the police was Chandu, while he was getting a stolen car serviced by Shera. Only a few gang members knew that Chandu had taken the vehicle for servicing. Shera suspected Happy of foul play.

Meanwhile, Rocky was busy 'educating' the youngsters about risky crimes like robberies, as he wanted to contest elections, and did not want fresh trouble. He convinced Shera and the others to bury the hatchet with Happy. However, once developed, the cracks only widened. One day, Shera killed Happy and danced on the bonnet of his car. Rocky was livid. He had already lost the elections and was in jail, but he seemed to be adamant about contesting the next Assembly election in 2017. Being Dimpy's protégé, he could not digest Shera doing something he had asked him not to do. He had wanted Shera to lie low for a while. Rocky's fiefdom, his name and his control over the gangster were under threat.

A month later, Shera Khuban was killed in a police encounter. Jaipal and Vicky were livid with Rocky. They suspected he had informed the police about Shera's hideout. Just a few days before Shera's murder, Rocky and another gangster-turned-politician-turned-social-activist, Lakha Sidhana, had organized a dinner for Shera. Shera's girlfriend had accompanied him. Vicky was also present at the dinner. Jaipal and Vicky believed Rocky had planned the dinner only to confirm Shera's hideout.

In the Punjab gangland, *mukhbari* or snitching is a cardinal sin.

No killing of a friend or gang member is forgotten in the ruthless world of gangsters. If you live by the gun, you perish by the gun. These gangsters commit crimes together, flee together, stay in hiding together. They have each other's back. Trust becomes the glue of their friendship—stronger than even real blood.

And on the betrayal of trust, blood can be shed.

◆

Rocky lived life on a high, surrounded by his supporters and enjoying political patronage. He often spent weekends at hill stations. He had bought some vehicles too, including a car and a Mahindra Scorpio. Invariably, the registration number of each vehicle was 9091. He had been told by a Bangalore-based astrologer that he would be safe in a vehicle with this number. As it turned out, this was but mere superstition, and superstitions do not protect anyone.

On 30 April 2016, Rocky Fazilka was returning from Shimla. He often stopped at a juice vendor near Solan. He was travelling in a Toyota Fortuner (PB 04U 9091). His gunman Parampal was driving it. His cousin Harpreet Singh was on the rear seat. Harpreet was a nephew of Rocky's paternal uncle's wife. As mentioned earlier, the paternal uncle and his wife were childless and had declared Rocky as their adopted son.

Another team of bodyguards tailed them in a Scorpio since Shimla, but near Timber Trail in Parwanoo, somehow, it was left behind. Harpreet got the car stopped here, complaining of nausea. He had just boarded the vehicle back when Jaipal came out in front of Rocky with a .9mm pistol and shot him dead.

Within hours, there were celebratory posts on the Facebook pages of rival gangsters.

Gurpreet Sekhon, who was facing trial in the murder case of another Sukha Kahlwan, rejoiced: '*Ajj sade veer Shera Khuban da badla pura ho gya. Ah peya vadda badmash Rocky Fazilka.*' (Today, we have avenged the killing of our brother Shera Khuban. The so-called big don Rocky Fazilka is dead now.)

Vicky Gounder chuckled at the murder. In a Facebook post, he rubbed it in that Rocky Fazilka had finally become an MLA—*Aah banata MLA*, he wrote in Punjabi. In the same post, he also threatened SSP Swapan Sharma, an IPS officer—who had arrested Vicky earlier and had carried out other anti-gangster operations as well. Vicky said the SSP wanted to pin him down and rub his nose to the ground. Instead, 'I (Vicky) have done this with his friend Rocky.'[2]

Another gangster, Jodha Kothaguru, lodged in the high-security Nabha Jail with Gurpreet, termed Rocky's murder a revenge killing. 'If you will kill our friend (Shera Khuban), we will kill many of yours. Our history (referring to Punjab's tales of valour and revenge) is testimony to this,' gloated Jodha on Facebook.

Based on the statement of Rocky Fazilka's driver Parampal, Solan Police booked Jaipal and unknown accomplices for the murder. Also booked on the basis of a suspicious cell phone location were three youths from Patiala who had no previous criminal record. It seems they were in the vicinity of Rocky's car for a long time during the journey from Shimla to Parwaano.

The three youths turned out to be innocent and were later acquitted by the court.

No one else was arrested. The police believed that the murder of gangster Happy Deora at the hands of Shera Khuban was an isolated case of enmity among gangsters.

But Rocky Fazilka's killing had wider ramifications, and marked the beginning of a ruthless gang war that would snuff out many a young and promising lives in Punjab.

---

[2]'Rockey Murder: Jailed Gangsters take shots on FB', *The Times of India*, 2 May 2016, https://tinyurl.com/3as2shax. Accessed on 16 December 2025.

3

Shera Khuban

IF EVEN SOME OF THE hopes pinned on Gurshaheed Singh alias Shera Khuban had come true, he would have been feted as a champion athlete, and on the basis of his achievements in sports, would have landed a secure government job. No one would have been surprised had he even become a police officer through the sports quota, like hockey Olympian Gagan Ajit Singh, or the Indian women's cricket team captain Harmanpreet Kaur.

There was a strong possibility of him becoming a coach and training young talent. Things could have been different from what often happens to youth like him when they don't get their due.

Named Gurshaheed Singh at birth, he was born in Khuban in Abohar Tehsil not far from Badal village—the native place and a seat of power in Punjab for five-time chief minister the late Parkash Singh Badal.

Gurshaheed means 'one who achieved martyrdom on the path shown by his guru.' In Punjab, a *shaheed* (martyr) is one who sacrificed his life to uphold justice, righteousness, or for the welfare of others. Shaheeds are celebrated for their courage, resilience, and unwavering commitment to their beliefs, especially religious beliefs, and loyalty to their motherland and family. Numerous gurudwaras, called 'gurudwara shaheedan,' have been built in memory of Sikh Gurus, their children and followers who did not submit to the diktats of Muslim rulers, and chose to die than to convert to Islam.

Their supreme sacrifice permeated the Punjabi culture. Anyone who died fighting for India's independence is revered in Punjab across caste and community. Likewise, Bhagat Singh, Rajguru and Sukhdev, branded as 'revolutionary terrorists' by the British, and who achieved martyrdom, are held in high esteem. It is also common to see memorial gates at the entrance of villages in Punjab, showcasing photographs and particulars of martyrs from the village. Such gates, and even roads and streets, are named after the shaheeds.

In such a culture, if someone prophesied that a great shaheed would be born into a family, it was considered a blessing instead of being a cause for sadness over the fate of the child. The courage and strength of a martyr are worn like a badge of honour in the martial culture of Punjab.

When Jarnail Singh, father of Shera Khuban, was told that a shaheed would be born to him, he was overjoyed.

'I was not even married when a Nihang Baba prophesied the birth of my son. It so happened that I was visiting Nanaksar Thath near Jagraon in Ludhiana. While passing in front of the stalls selling religious symbols besides toys, a Nihang Sikh offered a mouth organ for my children.'

That was in 1974, years before Shera's birth in 1988. 'It was a plastic mouth organ orange in colour, which is still popular among kids. He handed it to me saying I will not just have a son but a great one who will earn much fame. He will be a shaheed.'

Singh recalls that while he did not take the prophecy seriously, he never forgot it either. 'When my son was born, I named him Gurshaheed Singh. His mother called him Happy.

Later, when his coaches saw him throwing the hammer far better than other youngsters of his age, and with a loud roar, they named him Shera—lion. Then on, while the journey to becoming Shera Khuban turned into an ordeal which claimed his life, we are still living with it.'

A wrestler in his days, Singh had taken up a contract of levelling dunes. Khuban village is situated in the semi-arid zone of Punjab's Malwa region adjoining Haryana, and the desert state of Rajasthan. Sand dunes and even mounds came in the way of cultivation. Singh and his team removed the dunes with tractors and other equipment, and levelled the fields. The work just sounded easy. While tackling a stubborn and high mound, Singh's tractor overturned. 'Hardly any bone was left intact in my body. I was bedridden for two years. I promised myself I would make my son so strong and hardy that nothing would break him.'

After two daughters, a son was born. In those days, the sex-determination test was not banned. When Singh learnt that his wife was pregnant with a male child, he was ecstatic. Patriarchal Punjab celebrates the birth of a son, the heir of ancestral property, the one who will carry the family name forward.

Singh wanted his son to be strong like Gaama Pehalwan or Dara Singh—two famous wrestlers who were the benchmark of strength, and built like Hercules in classical mythology. Singh ordered a strict diet for his wife. He brought home 30 kg of almonds and other dry fruits, and 15 kg of desi ghee, besides feeding her seasonal fruits and meat. 'You will nurture him with these,' he had decided on behalf of both the parents.

'When Gurshaheed was born, he weighed 5.4 kg—far above the average 3 to 3.5 kg. I knew that the strong son I dreamt about and was told about had taken birth.

'We fed him juice, soup, milk and lassi. Eating one to two kg of meat was normal for my son. When he developed muscles, I trained him to be a wrestler. His body was so hard, you couldn't pinch him. There was no loose fat anywhere. It was like attempting to dent a boulder with a feather.' Singh talks about all this with pride in several interviews.

Jarnail Singh's great-grandfather owned 1,100 acres of land in Lahore, decades before India was partitioned to carve out Pakistan in 1947. By that time, Singh's father owned approximately 150 acres, as the huge landholding had been divided up among the grandfather and grand-uncles. The Jat Sikh family was among millions who had to forcibly migrate to India during Partition. Singh recalls spending his young days in refugee camp in Jagraon. Later, they were allotted land in Khuban village. The family did not have documents to claim the loss of 150 acres.

Despite all the hardships, Singh remained a devout Sikh, and would often visit the Golden Temple in Amritsar to pay obeisance and offer his gratitude to the Almighty for whatever he had. He visited the shrine annually in thanksgiving for the birth of Gurshaheed.

In 2009, a group of victims of the 1984 Union Carbide gas leak in Bhopal visited the Golden Temple. Among them were the two siblings who had been born blind as a lingering effect of that poisonous gas. Jarnail Singh was moved by their plight and began supporting the family financially, sending money every month; the children visited him often.

Years later, when Punjab Police, on the trail of gangster Shera Khuban, raided his house, they picked up Singh; at the time, the blind children and their parents were visiting him. 'I was mistreated and will never forget the humiliation at the hands of the police that day. They painted us all as criminals because Shera had killed someone. The police and the system never bothered about why Gurshaheed became Shera Khuban, the gangster.'

At 5'11", it wasn't just Shera's physique that set him apart. He had developed good looks too—a wide forehead partially covered with a rebellious strand of hair, and small but penetrating eyes with dark-brown irises on a sea of white. His lips were neither plump nor thin, and he had a beard that was neither thick nor imposing. Holding a pistol in his photos, the flexed forearm muscles provided a hint of his physique hidden behind carelessly worn clothes.

In short, his face was nothing like the brute force his body suggested. He wore a gentle smile over a calm demeanour.

Singh took Shera to local sports clubs seeking their advice on the sport he should train for. They first thought of wrestling but later settled for hammer throw. In this sport, the athlete throws a metal ball attached to a steel wire. The athlete spins the metal ball a few times to build up the momentum before releasing the steel wire to fling the ball. The one who throws the farthest, wins.

At the age of 16, Shera threw the hammer 42 metres—an exceptional mark especially because he used a 16-pound (7.26 kg) metal ball, the weight usually reserved for senior athletes. Juniors under 19 competed with an 11-pound (5 kg) metal ball.

Shera threw the ball this far in the trial for the Punjab Sports Academy. By then, he had already won a number of tournaments at the district, inter-school and state levels. It was 2006, and the Punjab Government under Capt. Amarinder Singh of the Congress had announced a new sports policy to attract, train and nurture future champions who could shine at national and international levels.

This was an all-paid scholarship where the government sponsored the player's education, training, diet, boarding and lodging. These trials were part of the selection process for admission to the Punjab Sports Academy, the state's flagship initiative to build a pipeline of sporting talent.

In the first trials, as mentioned earlier, Shera threw the 11-pound hammer 42 metres. For his age, this was impressive as he had only local training. However, he was not selected. To their shock, the seat for the athlete in this category was kept vacant.

Singh met the Director Sports, Punjab. He wasn't too impressed but allowed a re-trial. Shera then went to Jalandhar for the trials. He was given 16-pound hammers with the excuse that only this weight was available. He threw it 44 metres. 'This was the first time that he had tried this heavy a weight,' recalls Singh. But he was not selected.

Shera lost his temper at the treatment meted out to him but his father prevailed upon him to be patient.

The father-son duo did not give up. Singh contacted a coach in Ludhiana, rented a house near the railway station, and moved there with Shera. While Shera trained, Singh's mother prepared food for him, ensuring that his special diet of dry fruits and meat continued uninterrupted.

A few weeks later, more players from the state joined the coach, and Singh accommodated them in the rented house. He then hired a cook as he had to return home and take care of the crops during harvesting.

It seems that a rival group called the Dhodhi Group of Athletes—wrestlers and hammer and discus throwers—were closer to the sports authorities. One day, this group had an argument with Shera while practising, and beat him to pulp with baseball bats and hockey sticks. According to his father, they wanted to finish off his sports career by breaking his limbs. But Shera survived without fractures, though he ended up with 32 stitches on his head. Fortunately, some jawans of the Border Security Forces, who were also sportsmen, saved his life. They and the Dhodhi Group rushed Shera to the civil hospital. At the hospital, Shera, fearing that the Dhodhi Group may cause him more harm or use their influence to disallow a proper medico-legal report, called up some of his friends in Chandigarh. These friends were mainly students from Guru Gobind Singh Khalsa College, Chandigarh. Shera had met them at a sports tournament earlier.

Within a couple of hours, the friends landed up in cars and jeeps and thrashed Shera's assailants in the hospital itself. The wounded and Shera were admitted in the same ward.

Among the friends who had come to help Shera was Jaipal Bhullar, the son of a cop. A hammer thrower himself, Jaipal hailed from Ferozepore. Taking help from his Chandigarh friends that day proved life-altering for Shera. First, he was angry with the sports authorities for denying him admission in the Sport Academy. Then he became indebted to the youths who had came all the way from Chandigarh to help him.

Nearly two weeks later, Shera informed his parents about the fight. Singh scolded him for getting into such a mess and not informing his parents. 'We sent you to win medals, not to get wounds on your body,' Singh rebuked him, trying to heal his injuries with his gentle touch. Then, with the help of a Ludhiana Congress leader and other friends, Singh reached a compromise with the Dhodhi Group, which had sons of powerful police officials.

For several months, Shera stayed at home before wanting to return to the sports field again. Singh too wanted his son to forget the 'one-off' brawl and the rejection by the Sports

Academy. He took Shera to sports coaches in Haryana and Rajasthan with the aim of keeping him away from Punjab.

Shera was welcomed everywhere as his hammer throw had greatly improved. But he did not adjust well to any place outside Punjab.

Time went by and Jarnail moved his son to Chandigarh, to Guru Gobind Singh Khalsa College, at the behest of a woman relative who was a lecturer there. Shera started training again. But as fate would have it, the friends who came to his help against the Dhodhi Group were also sportsmen and trained with him.

Shera starting hanging out with them. In this new world, where he had faced rejection, injustice, assaults on body and mind, the new group of friends took him into their fold.

Among others were Jaipal Bhullar, and Tinu Rana, another name in the underworld. Both Jaipal and Tinu were sons of cops, one in Punjab Police and another with Chandigarh Police.

The desire to conform to the expectations of such a group that was angry with the world for a host of reasons—legitimate or otherwise—often compel youths like Shera to go to extremes. To gain the 'respect' of the group or to even remain a follower, youths often take to ways that go against societal norms. Shera was sucked into a world neither he nor his parents had dreamt of. He just wanted to fit in.

Unknown to Shera, according to the claims of his father, Jaipal's group was already involved in criminal activities since 2007. They had been involved in snatchings, robberies and carjackings.

◆

It was 29 January 2009. Shera was in second year of college, studying for a Bachelor's degree. According to Shera's statement to the police and what his father claimed, Jaipal told Shera to meet them in Ludhiana early morning. Jaipal and two others arrived in a white Hyundai Accent.

'We have some work in Barnala,' they told him. Later, Shera told his father that he could not say no to them, nor did he ask any questions.

At Barnala, they stopped near the bus stand and waited for another group of friends to arrive. It did not.

Meanwhile, two constables alighted from a bus that had arrived from Bathinda. A handcuffed youth was with them.

'Do you see them?' Jaipal asked Shera.

He nodded.

'That is Rajiv Raja. The media call him Jewel Killer,' Jaipal updated him. Then came the chilling direction, 'We are here to rescue him.'

'What?'

'Yes. We were supposed to keep an eye on the developments but the main group that was meant to execute Raja's escape has ditched us. It is time you became a man and proved your mettle.' Jaipal was direct and cold.

Shera told his father that Jaipal's exact words were: '*Munde ton mard ban ke dekha.*' (Time you become a man from a boy).

Shera got out of the car. His chest swelled, and testosterone rushed to his head. He walked straight up to the two constables sitting on chairs next to the handcuffed Rajiv. He delivered one blow to the first constable close to Rajiv and then another blow to the second. Both cops collapsed unconscious.

Shera grabbed Rajiv's arm and pulled him towards the car. The group sped away after having pulled off a daring escape from police custody in broad daylight.

As long as he lived, he would repent succumbing to peer pressure that fateful day. 'He broke down a number of times before me, in jail, and at home in the dead of night, wishing he had said no that day,' recalls Jarnail Singh.

Rajiv had been involved in a sensational triple murder case of a jeweller family in Ludhiana. He had looted many other jewellers too.

A shell-shocked Punjab Police went berserk tracking Rajiv and the men who had freed him from police custody.

◆

Six months later, Rajiv was nabbed in Kurukshetra. Shera was apprehended in Chandigarh.

Singh paused before talking about the first time he saw Shera in police custody. 'One of our relatives is an Assistant Sub-Inspector in Punjab Police. He called me that day to ask what is the name of my son. Relatives called him only by his nickname Happy. I told him it is Gurshaheed Singh. He asked if he is also known as Shera.

'When I replied in the affirmative, he went quiet for what seemed like an eternity to me. My heart was thumping in my chest. I imagined something bad happened to Shera and it had.

'"What happened. Tell me fast," I was begging to know.

'"He is ok. Just that he has fallen into bad company. He is in the custody of Chandigarh Police. We have to go there immediately."

'My son, who I dreamt would be standing smiling victoriously on podiums at national and international levels, with the national anthem of India playing in the background, was sitting on his haunches with other "criminals" in the room of Inspector Ranjit Singh when we reached the police station in Chandigarh.

'My body and mind gave way. I collapsed on the floor. This was too unbearable for me.

'When I came around, I was lying on the bench, while Shera and the cops were standing around me.

'"Bapu, muster up your courage. The clock can't turn back. This is the new reality," Shera said with conviction.

'When they whisked him away to the lock-up, preparing documents, Inspector Singh consoled me first and then in a cold voice said, "Save your son from the hell he is sinking into. Now is the moment. But having seen many of his kind, I am telling you today that he will become an Inaami gangster, whose posters will be circulated, and he will carry a cash reward for his arrest or his head."

'As I looked bewildered, Inspector Singh told me, "I will not hide from you. The police had to use methods to extract information. While others cried for mercy, Shera laughed at us. I realized soon that beating has no effect on him. I had to strike up a conversation with love and understanding and then he told me his life story. This is his first major crime. It is now or never for you."'

'I wish I had not gone to Barnala that day,' Shera would often tell his father later, breaking down and sobbing helplessly. But back in the company of criminals, Shera would become Shera Khuban again. And his tribe and clout grew.

In Burail Jail, he met Rocky Fazilka—the top don of Punjab at that time. Rocky, Jaipal, Happy and Shera along with a drug addict Chandu from Ferozepore made a formidable group, carrying out robberies, bank heists, extortions, and threats to others. (*See* Chapter Two)

◆

In September 2011, after nearly two years, Shera Khuban was released on bail. The release from jail usually happens late in the evening due to the verification of documents. Jarnail

Singh was waiting outside the jail to take his son home in the hope that he could still save him from the vortex of crime and criminals that he had been sucked into. But he was mistaken.

'Daddy, I will come home tomorrow. You prepare food for 2,000 persons. I have to go now,' he said, briefly hugging his father, who with his grey hair and pain on his face broke down. But Shera had no time. 'Have courage, father,' he whispered before climbing into a waiting white Toyota Fortuner. Singh stood there helplessly, wondering if he should worry about the gun-toting persons in the car or about the party that Shera had asked him to throw the next day.

The following day was like a village mela. 'Not 2,000, more than 2,500 people joined us in the revelry. Shera reached there in a large cavalcade—some say 400 cars, others say 700. I don't know but there was no road or street in the village where you could not see rows of cars parked.'

Among those who accompanied Shera home were his followers on social media and several gangsters including Rocky Fazilka and a number of politicians from the Congress and Akalis. 'People recollected such frenzy only on Dimpy Chandbhan's and Rocky Fazilka's release from jail, and said Shera had surpassed even them. I could not see any ganglord from Uttar Pradesh though. People were clicking photos with my son. They were gifting him fruits, dry fruits, clothes and laddoos. He was garlanded hundreds of times over. Under other circumstances, I would have been proud, but my heart was sinking. I could feel the impending doom.'

◆

Not just men, there were women too—mainly female relatives, or womenfolk from the village, who came to help attend to the unprecedented number of guests. Some brought milk, others cheese, and some butter. Villagers also dumped a trolley of dry wood at the hurriedly set-up open kitchen in the grounds of the community hall. Most women gathered there to help in the cooking. Some relatives, their friends or members of the extended family gathered in Shera's house. They had no fear in being associated with a gangster.

Soon, word about the huge following and influence that Shera had spread like wildfire. People started coming to Shera, or in his absence, to his father to sort out disputes. Politicians often dropped in. Shera's followers meant voters for them. Shera's influence could keep rival politicians in check.

Among those deeply influenced by Shera was Namjeet Kaur (name changed), a distant relative of Shera's *bua* (paternal aunt). She was floored at the very sight of the gangster at a family function in Urlana village near Patran town, situated near the Punjab-Haryana border.

'People feared him. But he was so soft-spoken. There was truth in his eyes. I felt only I knew the real him,' she would tell cops later. Shera fell into her arms. Love blossomed amidst crime and chaos in their lives. Tall and slim, Namjeet matched Shera's courage and built with her energy, calm and earthen beauty. She belonged to Malout town in Muktsar District, some 25 km west of Khuban village.

Namjeet was not a typical rural girl waiting to get married according to her parents' wishes. She was a career woman—a lecturer in physics—and taught in a college. Her two siblings and parents had moved to Canada trying for Permanent Resident status. The family had taken loans to fulfil the Canadian dreams and Namjeet was paying off those loans. She had once dreamt of being an IAS or an IPS officer, but could not. She wanted to prepare for the Punjab Civil Services (PCS) exams but could never find time to study because of the job. Shera arrived in her life like a godsend. 'Live your dream. Prepare for the civil services. My life is doomed. I will be happy if I could help one to follow the good path,' he told her.

He gave her emotional and financial help. Shera was getting regular funds from different sources and had opened a paying guest accommodation in Chandigarh for regular income. How Shera got the funds to buy such a costly property in Chandigarh is anybody's guess.

The place was a perfect hideout for the gang. Often, they would commit a crime and hide there. Namjeet often waited for him there. They would sometimes go up the hills for a short rendezvous.

Namjeet did not agree to talk about her life with Shera.

According to the police, they got married secretly. When the police swooped down on Shera, she was with him, wearing a white top and sky-blue jeans and *churas* (wedding bangles). Later, she stated to the police that she was not married to Shera and was just a distant relative. She even claimed Shera had kidnapped her and held her forcefully. But the police found phone calls, messages and scores of photographs of the 'happy couple'. But more about that later.

◆

The 2012 Assembly elections turned out to be a fierce battle between incumbent Chief Minister Parkash Singh Badal—head of the Badal family—and ex-Chief Minister Capt. Amarinder Singh of the Congress. The rivalry was bitter. As Chief Minister from 2002 to 2007, Capt. Amarinder Singh had thrown the Badals, including Parkash Singh Badal, his wife Surinder Kaur, and son Sukhbir Singh in jail on corruption charges during Badal's rule earlier. When the Badals came back to power, they returned the gesture but in greater measure. They put behind bars Capt. Amarinder Singh's trusted personal staff and several other Congress leaders. More than 5,000 cases against Congressmen were lodged. In 2017, after becoming Chief Minister, Capt. Amarinder Singh set up a special Commission of Inquiry into the false cases registered during Badal's rule of ten years as Chief Minister of Punjab from 2007 to 2017.

The 2012 Assembly elections were fought at the peak of this bitter rivalry. It was a no-holds-barred election. Both the parties left nothing to chance to win the elections. They used musclemen and even gangsters.

One such leader was from Ferozepore, who had an army of musclemen. He had brought a huge cavalcade of vehicles and men for Shera Khuban's welcome party in his village when he was released on bail some seven months ago. Shera along with Jaipal, Chandu and others reached Ferozepore and took over the campaign. Such was Shera's influence that more crowds showed up at Congress rallies than for the rival Akalis. Shera had been especially chosen to arrange crowds for a rally for the Gandhi family scion Rahul Gandhi. Unknown to Shera at that time, many youths were attracted to his charisma and were eager to follow in his footsteps, even in the world of crime. One such youth, who emerged from that political rally and made a big name in the world of gangsters, was Gurpreet Sekhon.

Shera was impressed by Gurpreet's management skills at the rally. Organized on 26 January, Rahul Gandhi had come to boost the party's fortunes. Ferozepore is a border district, just next to Hussainiwala border point with Pakistan. This is also the district where the Sutlej and the Beas rivers' confluence form a giant lake and wetlands known as Harike Wetland. The water body attracts not just migratory birds from as far as Siberia but also tourists who come to see dolphins and alligators, besides enjoying quality fishes. Sukhbir Singh Badal, son of Parkash Singh Badal, infamously announced boosting tourism further by introducing amphibian buses that float like boats in the water. The scheme never worked.

Shera grew quite fond of Gurpreet Sekhon and campaigned for Satkar Kaur, the Congress leader travelling in Sekhon's car. On voting day, they learnt that the Akalis and their musclemen were pressurizing voters.

Gupreet and an accomplice Chandu detailed the sequence of events in their statements to the police.

Chandu's presence in the story is telling, because he was far from an ordinary foot soldier. Born in 1984 in Ferozepore Cantt, Chandu was notorious in Punjab's underworld where he would play a supporting role in the life of many gangsters. Senior in age and experience to infamous gangsters like Shera, Chandu's trajectory from a drug-addicted youth to a seasoned gangster reflects the broader decay wrought by narcotics in Punjab—a land once celebrated for its valour and agricultural abundance. His descent into a world of crime began at 16, when he dropped out of college and succumbed to addiction, following the familiar pattern of peer-induced drug use, theft, and eventual entanglement with the police.

His time in jail only strengthened his criminal ties, connecting him with emerging figures like Happy Deora, Rocky Fazilka, and Shera Khuban. These alliances led him into a web of violent crimes, including highway robberies, bank heists, and arms lootings.

His connections extended to politics as well; he supported Congress leaders during the 2007 and 2012 elections, even leveraging his ties with the Shera Khuban gang to help the campaign. That's how Shera reached Ferozepore—to organize a campaign for Congress leader Rahul Gandhi, and provide services for the rally.

With Gurpreet Sekhon, Shera controlled the area. But on polling day, the Akalis sent out their musclemen. In Piareana village, the feared clash erupted. Shera got a call that rival musclemen had taken over a poll booth in the village. He reached there, and in the clash, gunshots were fired. A voter died due to a bullet injury. Shera and his gang were booked.

The Akalis were in power and to make matters worse for the Congress leaders and the Shera Khuban gang, the Akalis won the elections and formed the government again.

Karmiti Sekhon, an influential landlord of Ferozepore, belonging to Karmiti village, was a frontrunner Akali supporter. He and Shera became sworn enemies.

◆

Almost when Shera was training hard to break records in hammer throw, a young man named Kuldeep Chahal in Uljhana village in Sirsa, Haryana, was rising early to reach the wrestler's *akhara* and do *varjish* or exercises religiously. Like Shera, he was an aspiring sportsman but did not let his academics slide. His physique and sports achievements landed him the job of Sub-Inspector in Chandigarh Police. But he was not satisfied with that. So, while Rocky Fazilka was rebulding his empire after the killing of Dimpy Chandbhan in 2006, and Shera Khuban, Chandu, Jaipal Bhullar and Gurpreet Sekhon were gaining notoriety in the underworld, Kuldeep was relentlessly pursuing his dream to be a police officer. Yes, he was already a cop but he wanted to be an IPS officer, not a non-gazetted-rank police official (ranks below DSP are non-gazetted). In 2009, he cleared the IPS and was among the first officers to arrest and interrogate Lawrence Bishnoi, who had just started spreading his wings in the world of crime. Later, Kuldeep also nabbed one Aman Sakoda, a notorious conman having links with several politicians, police officers including of the rank of Director General of Police, and several civil administration officers.

Shortly after the Punjab Assembly elections and the formation of the Akali-BJP government, Kuldeep was posted as Superintendent of Police (SP), Bathinda. Among other criminals, he had got the file of Shera Khuban to work on. Shera's village was less than 50 km from Bathinda. At that time, he was a fugitive. On September 9, an alert was sounded in Punjab, Haryana and Himachal Pradesh about Shera Khuban and his gang, who had carried out fresh robberies in and around Chandigarh. The city is situated at the meeting point of the three states. This particular alert was about a firing incident in Sector 35 market in Chandigarh. It was alleged that Shera Khuban and his group had fired shots in the air after an altercation.

But Shera's whereabouts were unknown—he had vanished. Another IPS officer, Promod Ban, who would later become head of the specialized Anti-Gangster Task Force (AGTF) in 2022, was posted as DIG of Bathinda Range. He received information that Shera could be hiding in Bathinda. Bathinda SSP Sukchain Singh Gill, who later became the main police spokesperson of the AAP Government and SP Kuldeep Chahal, set up police barricades and activated intelligence cells and informers to get some clues on him. But to no avail.

Late evening, 11 September, Kuldeep returned to his rented accommodation in Kamla Nehru Colony. 'I was pretty exhausted after the day-long raids and brainstorming meetings. Shera had become a danger to public life and property. The brief to us was to be on high alert as he was prone to open fire on the slightest suspicion,' Kuldeep told this writer.

Kuldeep had just alighted from the Maruti Gypsy outside his house when a Toyota Fortuner drew up at a distance. Shera Khuban stepped out of it. Kuldeep and his security guards did not notice him immediately and casually walked away from the car, which was a few feet behind the entrance gate to his rented accommodation. They had hardly moved a few steps, when Shera stopped in his tracks for a second and their gaze met. 'Without losing a moment, Shera opened fire at the police party,' said Kuldeep. And the police returned fire. Kuldeep maintained this sequence of events to the media and later to an officer who conducted a judicial inquiry into the encounter.

Shera died on the spot.

Amidst the chaos of several police teams that arrived at the spot, apart from the media and public, no one noticed Namjeet Kaur. She saw everything from the first floor of the rented house she lived in as Shera Khuban's 'wife'. Only when she tried to slip out later did the police notice her. In her statement to the police about her proximity to the gangster, Namjeet said Shera met her at a function in Urlana village near Patran in Haryana.

She told police she had discussed her financial problems and those of her family members with Shera. Shera had assured her of all possible help. The girl had also been impressed by Shera's luxury vehicles. He also promised to give money to help Namjeet clear the PCS examinations and meet the expenses incurred on the coaching. Namjeet did appear in the Punjab Civil Services (PCS) exam but failed to clear it.

About 28 years old, Namjeet had a Master's in physics, and had worked in a multinational mobile company in Chandigarh. Namjeet claims to be working as a lecturer at a Polytechnic College in Bathinda.

Namjeet was jailed for four years. After her release from the jail, she remarried.

One man had assembled in the crowd after the encounter—Shera Khuban's closest aide, Vicky Gounder, another sportsman who dreamt of making a name in the field of sports but ended up a gangster. Vicky saw everything that evening. He also saw Namjeet Kaur wailing. She was particularly agitated at the sight of a man in a white kurta pyjama who was rubbing shoulders with the cops—Karmiti Sekhon. Years later, Neeta Deol, a close gangster friend of Vicky's, would reveal in a media interview with journalist Paramjit Bariana that Karmiti had slapped Namjeet a couple of times, and told her how Shera had finally paid the price for killing his party worker years ago in Piareana village.

Vicky had to avenge that killing.

For Shera's father, life came to a standstill the day his son was killed in an encounter.

'My son was physically so fit that his body seemed to be cast in iron. I poured everything into him—discipline, strength, love. He never lacked a healthy diet or care. But I couldn't stop him from slipping away.

'In the end, my broad-shouldered, muscular boy—who once roared in the field of sports and made his rivals tremble—was reduced to ashes in an urn that I held in my hands.

'The same hands that had once cradled him as a newborn.

'I ache to hold him again, just once.

'I wish I could turn back the clock to the moment he picked up a gun.

'I wish I could rewrite the past.'

4

Jaipal Bhullar

IT WAS 13 MAY 2021. The walls of the conference hall in the Organized Crime Control Unit (OCCU) office at Punjab Police Intelligence headquarters in Mohali bore a chilling emblem of their mission: a forbidding backlit board showcasing Punjab's most infamous gangsters, their faces marked with stark symbols: a red X, yellow handcuffs, an aeroplane, or a green running-man emoji.

Each mark carried its own significance.

A red X signals that the criminal is dead—either 'neutralized' in a police encounter or at the hands of a rival.

Yellow handcuffs proclaim captivity—a gangster confined behind bars.

The aeroplane indicates a fugitive who has fled abroad.

The green running-man emoji is used for those who have escaped from custody or jumped bail. They are the most dangerous—active for several years, out there somewhere, planning or carrying out their next crime.

Similar boards, smaller and simpler, with a collage of mug shots of the 'most wanted' as well as 'eliminated' gangsters hung in the offices of the Inspector General, the SP, the Deputy Superintendent of Police (DSP) and the lower ranks, as a grim reminder of the goal of each unit—to catch or neutralize the dreaded criminals.

One name that towered above the rest on the chart was Jaipal Bhullar. He had a long moustache, stubble beard and cropped hair. His distinct feature—grey-black eyes—and the penetrating look seemed to dare 'catch me if you can'!

At 6'4", his powerful build once made him a hammer-throw champion in his hometown Ferozepore. He seemed all set to make a name for himself at the national and even international level in the sport. But the athlete fell from grace, trading his potential spotlight in sports for a life in crime.

For nearly eight years, Jaipal remained unseen, untouched, and unstoppable. In January 2013, he was last in custody, walking out of a Panchkula courtroom on bail in a robbery case.

Jaipal Bhullar would often emerge from nowhere with his gang, strike, and disappear. Cops would only learn later that the crime was Jaipal's handiwork through his 'signature' modus operandi, or if an associate was caught. His writ ran large over the entire state of Punjab, and even over Haryana, Rajasthan and Himachal. He had his hideouts, followers and networks all over these places, but nowhere was his terror more pronounced than on National Highway 44 that connected Delhi to Amritsar, and that passed through several big cities besides industrial towns. Jaipal was suspected to have a large network where men and young boys provided him hideouts, safe houses, vehicles, fake documents and possible targets as well.

The cops christened his gang 'Highway Gangsters'. He would waylay rich people in swanky vehicles and rob them of their belongings and the vehicle as well. Why wasn't he called a highway robber then? Because he would not stop at just robbing the people. He would ask the victims to take the gang along to their residences and then extort as much money as he could before letting the family go.

Unlike many of his counterparts, Jaipal avoided technology. Mobile phones, which give away the location, were discarded from his life. His operations were based on the old-world method of face-to-face communication, creating a web of secrecy that confounded law enforcement time and again. He would use public phones, even travelling 20 km in either direction of his hideout.

With meticulousely crafted fake identities, he wove an intricate web of safe houses across different states that seamlessly blended into cities and villages without leaving a trace. He donned turbans, sported short, cropped hair, and even wore a ponytail at times. His appearance changed like a chameleon's—long beard, stubble, clean-shaven, each look paired with a different style of moustache—a true master of disguise and deception. Bewildered cops often wondered how he pulled it off so flawlessly.

On 13 May 2021, the police got an opportunity—not exactly a rare slip-up on Jaipal's part, but more a stroke of luck for the cops.

Nabbing him, however, was no child's play. Officers of the OCCU needed to piece together those tiny, elusive clues left behind by Jaipal or his associates, in order to solve the puzzle of his whereabouts.

◆

Jaipal's birthplace, Ferozepore, which is less than 15 km from the Hussainiwala border with Pakistan, bears the weight of history and loss. Here, the Sutlej River flows into Pakistan, though merely as a trickle, symbolizing restricted freedom under the Indus Water Treaty that favours India's rights over this riverwater. Once a thriving town on the Delhi–Kasur–Lahore route, Ferozepore was undone by the hurried strokes of Sir Cyril Radcliffe's pen. Drawn without any real understanding of India's geography or culture, the new borders shattered lives. The partition of Punjab in August 1947 severed Ferozepore's ties with Kasur, draining Ferozepore of its vitality, supplanting its once bustling trade and flourishing camaraderie with nothing but emptiness. Decades later, the town is still struggling to recover its lost spirit, grappling with limited education, scant employment, and unfulfilled dreams.

'I could have imagined my son as anything but a gangster,' begins Bhupinder Singh, his voice quavering yet heavy with the weight of the years gone by. Dressed in a steel-grey kurta pyjama, the retired sub-inspector still stands tall; his 6'3" frame a shadow of the strength he once exuded. His salt-and-pepper hair and beard highlight his eyes that are an enigmatic blend of blue, grey, and black. 'My son… He had the same eyes as me. And he was an inch taller—6'4"', he says with a wisp of pride, soon eclipsed by sorrow.

The former officer scratches his head, his memory faltering as he pieces together fragments of the past. 'We belonged to Vichoya, our ancestral village,' he recalls. 'But those were dark days—terrorism had overtaken rural Punjab. Policemen were being slaughtered. I had no choice but to move my family to an urban area for their safety.'

In 1988, Singh relocated to Dasmesh Nagar in Ferozepore, amidst widespread turmoil in rural Punjab. He acquired a small plot of 900 sq. yd that cost him ₹23,500. It was a modest haven but a sanctuary nonetheless. The town was affordable, offering peace for his wife, their two sons, and a daughter. 'Life there was simple. But the countryside…the countryside was a battlefield,' he says, lowering his voice as he narrates the terrors of the 1980s—when parts of rural Punjab became strongholds for Khalistani militants. The insurgency claimed thousands of lives, including the lives of over 1,700 police officers.

Amidst the chaos, Singh recalls moments that shaped his son. 'Jaipal was a kind-hearted boy,' he says, his voice softening as he tells the story of a wounded donkey whom Jaipal had found when he was just eight. 'He bandaged its wounds, fed it fodder meant for our cattle, and refused to visit his maternal grandparents until I promised to take care of it. When he returned a week later, his first question was about the donkey. I lied, told him it had healed and had been taken away. He was relieved. That's the kind of boy he was.'

Jaipal's tenderness was coupled with strength. By the age of 14, he had grown into a robust teenager, and Singh, seeing potential in him, introduced him to wrestling. 'My grandfather, Deepa Pehalwan, was a wrestler,' Singh says. 'I thought Jaipal could carry forward that legacy.' And he did, excelling in competitions, until one fateful encounter changed everything.

It was during a wrestling event that Jaipal caught the eye of hammer-throw coach Mohan Singh Bhullar. 'Jaipal was sceptical, and so was I, but Coach Bhullar insisted he try hammer throw,' Singh recalls. With no prior experience, Jaipal flung the heavy iron ball further than many seasoned athletes. His natural talent was undeniable, and soon he was enrolled in the Speed Fund Academy—a prestigious institution in Ludhiana that honed young athletes for international glory. Singh supported his son every step of the way, unaware of the shadows looming on the horizon.

'Little did I know that the decision to send him to the gym would lead him into the darkest recesses of hell,' Singh says, his voice breaking.

It was at the gym in 2002 that Jaipal met Happy Deora, the 25-year-old son of ASI Des Raj. 'Happy was charismatic but dangerous. His father misused his position, and Happy followed suit. I warned Jaipal, but he came under Happy's influence.'

Both were fated to walk down shadowy paths.

Happy was a domineering figure who used his father's position like a weapon. 'Both father and son had airs, as if the world owed them reverence,' recalls Singh. Happy's charm was a double-edged sword; he knew how to patronize youngsters, bending their wills like metal in fire. Jaipal, though reserved and detached, found himself strongly drawn to Happy's allure.

Des Raj's shadow had loomed long before this fateful meeting. Once a head constable alongside Jaipal's father, their bond had frayed over disputes and matters pertaining to corruption. Des Raj, a greedy man, thrived on contested lands and properties, turning his fortune around with ill-gotten wealth. Once, Jaipal's father had slapped him in a fit of rage—an act of righteous anger over some bribes. This slap forged resentment, and became an ember that was fanned into a vindictive flame.

Meanwhile, Jaipal was carving out his own identity at the Speed Fund Academy. The academy was a symbol of hope, nurturing the dreams of talented athletes of representing India on the international stage some day. Jaipal showed promise, and his coach predicted record-breaking achievements.

Des Raj's life was seeped in discord and tragedy. His elder daughter perished under mysterious circumstances, amidst arguments over her choice of husband. His younger sister and her husband, entangled in Ludhiana's working-class chaos, ran a cinema hall in the heart of a migrant labour colony. Their family lived in constant discord, with brawls erupting even on celebratory events like weddings. Slaps and insults became the language of their disputes, further fuelling the storm.

And then came the darkest chapter of all. In 2003, Happy kidnapped Chirag, his own nephew, dragging Jaipal along into the web of crime. Together, they demanded a ransom of ₹1 crore—an audacious act of greed and folly. The law caught up swiftly, yet the consequences rippled through the families like cracks spreading across a sheet of glass.

Jaipal's father pleaded with Chirag's family, begging for mercy. 'My son's future is bright; he did not know of Happy's intent,' he argued. But the cries for forgiveness fell on deaf ears. Jaipal's promising arc in the Speed Fund Academy was overshadowed by this act of betrayal, as Des Raj's fiery temperament only worsened the outcome.

'What is worse is that all this happened just weeks before Jaipal was scheduled to move to Canada for studies. He had even got his visa,' rued the father. Darkness, it is said, does not simply descend—it creeps up stealthily, spreads its tentacles, and consumes all in its wake.

Tears glisten in Singh's eyes as he concludes, 'Jaipal was destined for greatness. His coach had said he could break national records. But one wrong turn…one bad influence… and his life was shattered. As a father, I blame myself. I wanted to protect him, guide him…but I failed.'

The Crime Spree

While the father begged the kidnapped child's family for forgiveness and turned to every political and police connections he had to save his son, Jaipal wasn't looking for salvation. He was plunging headlong into darkness.

Jail did not break him. It built him. His influence grew behind bars, and soon, Happy, his childhood friend, introduced him to Rajiv Raja, a gangster whose name carried weight far beyond prison walls. Together, they formed a crew.

Rajiv was ruthless. Released on bail in 2006, he wasted no time—three members of a family in Ludhiana were gunned down and a jeweller robbed. Then he was back behind bars. But the connection with Jaipal remained unshaken.

◆

Jaipal's inner circle grew steadily. There was Chandu, Ramandeep Romi, Bhupinder Singh Bhappi—all hardened criminals, ready for the next phase. They built a network across Punjab, Haryana, and Himachal Pradesh, renting houses to serve as safe havens and operational bases. Soon, these hideouts would become the backbone of their criminal empire. And then they went on a spree.

In April 2009, a Toyota Innova was hijacked at gunpoint, the owners stripped of their valuables, and the car driven to a safe house in Pathankot. The gang travelled in the stolen Innova with fake plates, preparing for their next hit.

Next, a black Mercedes E-220 was stolen near Kurukshetra, Haryana. Then they forced the Mercedes owner, a businessman, to drive them to his home in Panchkula. Just when they were ready to empty out the place, the alarm rang—immediately relatives and neighbours spotted them. Forced to abandon the Mercedes, the gang fled back to Pathankot.

Then they stole a Hyundai Verna near Nakodar. And the same routine followed. But the gang was getting restless. They weren't making enough money. Jaipal knew it was time for something bigger.

So it was a bank robbery in Panchkula, Haryana. For days, Shera Khuban and Tinu Rana scoped out Sector 20, Panchkula. When the moment arrived, they struck fast. A cool ₹15 lakh were stolen in minutes. They retreated to a safe house and lay low in silence before beginning to plan their next strike.

Chandu, Raja, and Bhappi roamed the Panchkula-Ambala-Delhi highway, stealing a Honda City and kidnapping the owner and the driver. A call went to Jaipal. After he arrived, the victims were dragged to the gang's Sector 43 hideout in Chandigarh and made to pay for their freedom—₹6 lakh, plus gold and silver. The group decided to slow down. It did not help.

Raja, Bhappi, and Romi were caught in Haryana. Jaipal, Shera, and Harinder tried robbing another bank in Mohali, but the haul was small.

In July 2009, after looting a businessman in Ludhiana, Jaipal and Shera were returning to their Chandigarh safe house. But unknown to them, the police had already captured a gang member, Tinu Rana—so they were waiting. The trap had been laid, and soon Jaipal and Shera were arrested.

For three years, Jaipal languished in jail, while Shera got bail early. Then Shera entered Punjab's political war. In the 2012 Assembly elections, he began campaigning for Congress candidates, organizing muscle power, rallying crowds, and keeping rivals in check.

Meanwhile, Jaipal and Happy Deora's friendship was under stress. Happy, once his closest ally, was slipping away. Happy had aligned himself with Rocky, the most powerful gangster-politician in Punjab. Jaipal watched everything unfold, but refused to follow Rocky.

Politics drove a wedge into the bond. Shera and Gurpreet were Congress supporters while Rocky and Happy supported the Akali Dal. Another gangster, Sukhmeet Sekhon Karmiti, stood with the Akalis. The fault lines grew deeper.

It was polling day—30 January 2012. Shera and his men stood by, waiting for orders from the Congress leaders. Then there was a call from Piareana village—Akali musclemen had attacked Congress leader Laddi Gehri's men. Shera and Gurpreet had arrived, guns drawn. The shootout was quick. A stray bullet claimed an innocent life.

The police went after Shera and his gang. As pressure mounted, Shera suspected Happy had turned against him. Happy had to go.

Late 2012 in Ferozepore, Happy sat in his car. Shera flitted like a shadow. The shots were precise, brutal, final. But it wasn't just Shera. Jaipal was in a jail but had known everything. He had been one of the planners.

In November 2012, the police killed Shera Khuban in an encounter. Jaipal was certain it had been Rocky's gang. More blood was spilled. Jaipal walked free after securing bail in 2013, never to be caught alive again.

Another Crime Spree Unfolds

Jaipal Bhullar and his gang were always planning their next move, plotting each crime with a mix of precision and aggression. This time, they set their sights on Rajasthan, a state known for its vast highways and bustling cities, offering both opportunities and challenges for organized criminals.

Their first major strike in Rajasthan was a carefully planned robbery at State Bank of Patiala in Kota. On the day of the robbery, Jaipal and his associates stormed into the bank, weapons drawn, ensuring that every person inside understood the gravity of the situation. Too terrified to resist the sudden attack, the employees were forced to comply, as the gang worked quickly, stuffing bags with ₹7 lakh in cash. The operation lasted only a few minutes, but it was executed with chilling efficiency.

Without wasting time, the gang escaped the city, heading back to Punjab, where their network was stronger and their safe houses offered refuge. Over the past few years, Jaipal had developed a system that allowed his gang to disappear into the shadows, evading the police while expanding their reach.

Two new members joined their ranks—Ranjot Singh Jodhan and Jagseer Seera. The gang's hideouts had fanned out, now including a rented flat in Chandigarh.

Chandigarh, widely known as The City Beautiful, was ideal for criminals looking to blend in. Unlike smaller towns with familiar faces, Chandigarh's streets were filled with people from all across North India, including Jammu and Kashmir, Ladakh, Himachal Pradesh, Punjab, Haryana, and Uttarakhand. Young professionals, students, businessmen, and labourers filled the city, making it easy for gang members to blend in, and slip unnoticed into the multi-ethnic crowds.

While Jaipal plotted new crimes, he could not forget old vendettas. The killing of Shera Khuban had left a deep wound, and Jaipal thirsted for revenge. His ultimate goal was to eliminate Rocky, the gangster-politician who had built his own empire. However, Jaipal wasn't the only one seeking vengeance. His close aide, Gurpreet Sekhon, nursed his own set of grudges.

Two names were high on Gurpreet's hit list—Sukhmeet Sekhon Karmiti and Lakha Sidhana. On 16 May 2013, the Jaipal gang attempted to kill Lakha Sidhana. The attack was well-planned and nearly successful, with multiple shooters aiming to take down their target. Lakha was hit by four bullets, and his body shredded by gunfire. Yet, somehow, he survived. One of his close aides was not as fortunate and died on the spot.

Over the years, Lakha turned to politics and social activism, becoming a vocal advocate for Punjab's rights.

Over time, he campaigned for issues such as promotion of the Punjabi language, fair distribution of river waters, and demand for Chandigarh to be officially transferred to Punjab.

Despite the failed attack on Lakha, Jaipal's gang remained determinded to settle scores, refusing to let their enemies get away unpunished.

Gangsters had a term for this kind of patient revenge—'fielding' a rival, meaning a target was under constant surveillance, his movements carefully monitored by informants in the gang. The enemy was never safe, never out of sight, and would eventually be executed when the time was right.

The moment arrived on 20 December 2013. The atmosphere at Khosa Dal Singh Wala village was festive. A dog show was on, drawing locals and prominent figures from the area. Among them was Sukhmeet Sekhon Karmiti, who had been invited as the chief guest. Jaipal's gang saw a golden opportunity.

A white Maruti Swift Dzire, stolen from Gurdaspur, rolled into the event. In it were four men—Jaipal Bhullar, Chandu, Vicky Gounder, and Tirath Dhilwan. Without hesitation, they opened fire, targeting Sukhmeet Sekhon Karmiti and his gunman, Vicky Kailash. Both men dropped dead instantly, even before they could react.

The crowd panicked, scrambling for cover, terrified that the killers might turn their weapons on them. To ensure no one pursued them, Jaipal and his men fired in the sky, sending a clear warning—any attempt to follow them would end badly. Then Jaipal and his gang vanished.

For days, they hid, waiting for the heat to die down. Then they moved to Jaipur, Rajasthan's capital, where they were greeted by another notorious associate—Paramvir Singh Hariana.

Paramvir was an expert in highway robberies, specifically targeting trucks transporting high-value cargo—zinc, copper, dry fruits, electronics—on the Delhi-Mumbai highway.

On 24 January 2014, Jaipal and his associates attacked a truck transporting copper, seizing control at gunpoint. However, the truck was equipped with GPS tracking, and within minutes, the police caught up, resulting in the arrest of Chandu and Paramvir. Jaipal, however, escaped once again. But Chandu wasn't done yet. Even from behind bars, he maintained an iron grip on operations, using smuggled phones to manipulate civilian contractors bidding for Military Engineering Services (MES) projects.

Ferozepore, home to a sprawling military cantonment, was his family's territory. Their influence in construction and logistical services tied to military infrastructure allowed Chandu to intimidate rival bidders, ensuring that his network controlled lucrative tenders. Too afraid to challenge him, many contractors simply withdrew their bids, allowing his people to dominate the contracts without competition.

In 2016, another battle erupted. Chandu, locked inside Amritsar Jail, received an ominous call—his gang member Akul Khatri had been kidnapped by the Davinder Bambiha gang.

Davinder's crew had ambushed Akul from Meerut and while bringing him back to Punjab, forced him to call and lure two more gang members—Lamma Patti and Bagga Khan—from Malerkotla into an ambush.

This was a gang war like no other—Rocky Fazilka and Lawrence Bishnoi's faction was clashing violently, in a savage turf war with Jaipal's gang. Chandu contacted Jaipal immediately, who assembled a rescue team—Tirath Dhilwan, Manoj Thakur, Sunny Khwajke, and even a jailed gangster, Sonu Kangla. Using Sonu as bait, Jaipal's men set a trap for

Davinder's crew. When the rival gang arrived with their three captives, Jaipal's team opened fire, managing to secure the release of their kidnapped members. Hours later, however, Davinder retaliated—Lamma Patti was killed.

Shera Khuban's Revenge

Looting banks, hijacking swank cars besides engaging in gunfights with rival gangsters, were Jaipal's bread and butter but standing up for his friends and taking revenge for wrongdoings against them seemed to nurture his soul. He had settled scores with Happy through his gangster friend Shera Khuban. He helped another gangster friend Gurpreet Sekhon take revenge against Sukhmeet Sekhon Karmiti. But the biggest revenge was yet to be taken—for the killing of Shera Khuban in a police encounter. Jaipal was not angry with the cops. He was angry with the person who had, or could have, leaked information about Shera's hideout to the police. And he suspected Rocky.

On 30 April 2016, Jaipal killed Jaswinder Singh alias Rocky Fazilka near Parwanoo, Himachal Pradesh. With this killing, which he boasted later through a post on social media, Jaipal Bhullar became the top gangster of Punjab.

He could stake claims to this distinction as he had dethroned Rocky, the topmost gangster, who despite becoming a politician, could not escape gang wars.

Dimpy Chandbhan killed Makhan Singh to rise on the Punjab gang scene. Rocky killed Dimpy to claim he was the most powerful. Rocky allegedly was involved in the killing of Shera in a police encounter. Jaipal killed Rocky.

After rival Rocky's murder, Jaipal had written in his Facebook post: *Abhi to khel shuru hua hai* (The game has just begun).

Ludhiana Gold Heist: The Most Audacious Crime Yet

The Jaipal Bhullar gang carried out numerous criminal operations—high-profile assassinations, bloody turf wars, kidnappings, and brazen highway robberies. But the next heist they planned was different from anything they had done before.

Their target? IIFL Gold Loan branch at Gill Road, Ludhiana—a gold financing institution known for storing large reserves of gold pledged by borrowers as collateral against loans. Banks held vast amounts of cash, but a gold loan branch was even more valuable. Instead of hard-to-move stacks of currency, these banks had solid gold—easy to smuggle, difficult to trace, and worth millions.

Jaipal's younger brother, Amritpal Bhullar, was actively involved in executing the plan, coordinating with Gagan Judge, a gangster who was quickly making a name for himself in the underworld. Alongside them were Pardeep Singh Gardiwal, Gursewak Singh alias Sewak, and several others—all handpicked for their expertise in planning and carrying out high-risk missions.

Unlike their usual operations, which often relied on impulse, intimidation, and sheer violence, this heist required precision, patience, and meticulous organization. The gang studied every detail of the branch in Ludhiana—from security routines and staff schedules to the positioning of cameras and the escape routes.

They weren't just looking for a quick cash grab—they wanted pure gold, the kind that would cement their wealth and influence indefinitely.

On the day of the heist, the gang members moved about like ghosts, their faces covered, their weapons concealed, yet ready for action. Every move was calculated, every step had been rehearsed in their minds over and over again.

Without hesitation, they stormed into the IIFL Gold Loan branch, their sudden presence sending shockwaves through the unsuspecting staff. The employees barely had time to react before the gang took control of the bank, issuing sharp commands, ensuring no resistance.

The gang did not waste time on small bills or loose cash; they went straight for the gold reserves, moving quickly, unlocking the safes and the storage units. Had they received inside information? The way they navigated the vault, cutting through security barriers with expert precision, suggested that they knew exactly what they were looking for.

In a matter of minutes, they had secured a staggering 30 kg of gold—a fortune in itself. Alongside the gold, they grabbed ₹3 lakh in cash, though that was pocket change compared to the worth of their true prize.

The crime was flawlessly executed, leaving no evidence, no fingerprints, no clues for law enforcement agencies to follow. By the time the police reached the scene, Jaipal and his crew had vanished into the maze of Ludhiana's streets, their escape so seamless that officers struggled to find any trace of their movements.

For months, investigators scoured Punjab's underground channels, trying to trace the stolen gold. They followed black-market leads, raided suspected hideouts, interrogated informants, but the gold had completely disappeared.

A few days later, cops caught Gagan Judge and recovered ₹30 lakh from him. This was just a minuscule amount compared to the market price of gold at that time. The price fluctuating from ₹24 to ₹32 lakh per kg meant that the gold that was looted was worth at least ₹7 crore.

The gold was never recovered.

Years later, in January 2025, the Faridkot police claimed that the stolen gold had somehow reached the hands of Khalistan activist Amritpal Singh, a figure who had risen to prominence in Punjab's separatist movement.

A key figure in Amritpal's inner circle was Gurpreet Singh of Hari Nau village in Faridkot. Gurpreet Singh was the treasurer of the controversial organization Waris Punjab De, headed by Amritpal. Gurpreet had discovered something shocking. Allegedly, he had uncovered proof that Amritpal had access to gold—stolen by Jaipal's gang years ago and kept in the custody of a man allegedly in Dubai. Gurpreet was allegedly shot dead by some shooters. The mystery of the gold is yet to be solved.

The Chase

13 May 2021

That day, in Khanna District, police officers were conducting routine checks on travellers along NH-44. ASI Sukhbir Singh and two constables were stationed at a checkpoint, scrutinizing vehicles. Such checks were a regular affair in Punjab, a state grappling with drug smuggling and the lingering shadows of terrorism. Between 1980 and 1996, Punjab endured 16 years of insurgency, fuelled by demands for Khalistan—a separate Sikh state—and supported by Pakistan. These routine checkpoints, or *nakka*s, were the police's frontline defence against gangsters, smugglers, and potential threats.

The officers inspected the documents of the vehicle, scrutinized the occupants, and occasionally asked them to open the car trunk. They searched for suspicious modifications—

hidden compartments often used to smuggle drugs or weapons. If anything raised suspicion, they would ask passengers to step out, question them further, or even frisk them.

That day, the officers flagged down a white Hyundai i20. Unbeknownst to them, the driver was Jassi Kharar, and his co-passenger was none other than Jaipal Bhullar. Jaipal's cropped hair and trimmed beard, paired with Ray-Ban sunglasses, concealed his identity.

ASI Sukhbir Singh asked the two young men to step out of the car. It was a hunch, he would later tell his seniors. The duo exchanged uneasy glances, their discomfort palpable. Sukhbir took the car keys and began questioning Jaipal, asking who he was and where they were headed. As he frisked Jaipal, he discovered a gun tucked into his jeans. Meanwhile, the constables were questioning Jassi.

Jaipal remained silent, his demeanour tense. When Sukhbir asked him to stretch his arms, Jaipal complied—only to suddenly lunge forward, landing a punch that sent the officer staggering. Recovering quickly, Sukhbir tried to grab him, but Jaipal, strong and agile, pushed him back and snatched his 9mm pistol. Jassi too took the cue and pushed the two cops, who were questioning him. He too snatched a pistol from one of the cops.

Jaipal and Jassi scrambled back into their car, but without the keys, they were trapped.

The stunned constables and other officers at the nakka rushed to assist. Amidst the confusion, Jaipal and Jassi exchanged a glance and bolted from the vehicle. Behind them, a queue of cars had formed, their drivers honking impatiently. Spotting a Honda City in the line, the duo forced the driver out at gunpoint. Intimidated by their bloodshot eyes and the sight of the weapon, the driver complied without offering resistance.

Jaipal and Jassi jumped into the Honda City, smashed through the checkpoint, and, in a bold move, took a U-turn, and sped away on the wrong lane into darkness, leaving behind a trail of chaos and disbelief. Jaipal took along the 9mm pistol of the ASI.

The incident set off alarm bells in Punjab Police. Police nakkas are meant to nab suspects, not for criminals to snatch weapons of the police and flee.

The tension in the Punjab Police headquarters was palpable. DGP Intelligence, Dinkar Gupta, who would later head the National Investigation Agency (NIA), India's premier investigation agency, was livid. He asked the OCCU to spring into action immediately.

The OCCU team, under ADGP Amit Prasad, decorated Assistant Inspector General (AIG) Gurmeet Singh Chauhan, and DSP Bikram Brar, tried to piece together the puzzle—who were these two men?

The team reached Khanna and took charge of the case. The Khanna Police had already done much spadework. They had searched the car that was abandoned near the police check post by the two men.

In all this haste, Jaipal had left behind a crucial clue—a wallet. In it, the driver's license named him as Rajpal Singh of Ferozepore. But the cops believed this was a fake identity.

The OCCU team turned to their most potent weapon—the Punjab Artificial Intelligence System (PAIS). This cutting-edge software, introduced in 2018, was equipped with facial recognition and smart glasses integration, allowing officers to scan crowds and identify suspects within seconds. The PAIS confirmed the man was indeed Jaipal, whose mastery over identities had helped him evade capture for far too long.

The resemblance between the license photo and Jaipal was

uncanny. Still, this was just the start. Jaipal could be anywhere and anyone, since the cops had also found digital cards for forging driving licenses—tools a smart criminal could use artfully.

The first thing the OCCU team did was to keep information about Jaipal's involvement at the Khanna Police check altercation a secret. This could lead the sharp unsuspecting criminal to commit another mistake.

Thereafter, the OCCU team combined human intelligence with technology. Drawing on a wide network of police personnel, criminals, and informers—a network that extended even into jails—the cops dug deep, searching for suspects both on the ground and among underground operatives. The cops focused on people who had had some connection with Jaipal in the past.

Several possible associates surfaced, but whom should they track? Acting on a hunch, they started looking for suspects in the vicinity of Khanna town. Jaipal had been travelling on the national highway connecting Khanna with Ludhiana. They perused the records, asked informers, and eventually zeroed in on Darshan of Sahauli village near Payal, which lay along the national highway. But he had already vanished.

In the next couple of days, the cops tracked Darshan's movements. They also kept an eye on other suspects. Would any of them meet Jaipal? Would Jaipal contact them?

Three days had already passed but there was still no clue about Jaipal's movements. Random searches, phone tracking, informers led the cops to some of Jaipal's suspected safe houses but he had vanished. Meanwhile, Darshan's web of movements included Ludhiana, a big city, and neighbouring mofussil towns like Payal, Dakha, and Jagraon. But Darshan was known to keep multiple phones.

On 16 May, the trail culminated in violence in Jagraon. Jagraon Police received a tip-off that some suspected liquor smugglers had been spotted in a Hyundai i10 near the town's grain market—an open rectangular space where farm produce, especially wheat and paddy, is brought for sale. At its centre is a raised cemented plinth covered by a shed. A wide road circles the shed, with rows of shops of *arhityas* (commission agents) built around it. Commission agents are middlemen between the farmers and the buyers—government and private purchasers. The market is abuzz with activity twice a year—a few weeks in April/May and in October/November. Otherwise, it is usually empty barring a few vegetable sellers. Wheat harvesting was long over and procurement of the produce was also at its fag end. There were not many people in the market.

A team of Jagraon Police comprising ASI Bhagwan Singh along with ASI Dalwinderjit Singh and two homeguards reached the market. They spotted the car in question and waited for some time, hoping for some activity. Eventually, a canter rolled past nearby, and two men stepped out of the vehicle.

The two ASIs went towards the car while the others walked towards the canter. The cops were in civies. They belonged to the CIA unit of the police district. (Every police district is divided into police stations and police posts, each with their limited jurisdictions—a given area in the district. A central agency called the Central Investigation Agency or CIA steps in to handle homicide, robbery, or when special raids are conducted to nab gangsters, bust drugs or liquor smuggling. To avoid easy detection by criminals, often they carry out raids in civies.)

Unknown to the police, Jaipal Bhullar and Jassi Kharar

were in the car and seemed to have guessed that the men in civies were cops. Before ASI Bhagwan Singh and ASI Dalwinderjit Singh could approach them, Jaipal and Jassi were out of the car. They took a red suitcase out of the car's trunk. The cops thought there was no need to hide their identities since they had to question the suspects. Dalwinderjit was asking questions while Bhagwan took out his mobile and took their photos. He wanted to check the photos on the PAIS system. Jaipal, fast as ever, seemed to have guessed it. He raised an alarm and his accomplice Jassi, a trigger-happy criminal always spoiling for a fight, fished out his pistol and fired. The two ASIs died on the spot. ASI Bhagwan Singh suffered a hole in the neck while ASI Dalwinderjit Singh fell down clutching his waist. Jaipal and Jassi charged towards the canter, challenging the other cops who were unarmed and thought better than to put up a fight. The criminals boarded the canter and sped away, taking with them the service weapons of the two dead ASIs.

Hours later, the OCCU team reached there, exasperated and frustrated at the loss of two lives. The scene baffled investigators. No drugs, no contraband, no immediate reason for the murder. Why had they fired? Why eliminate the ASIs in cold blood? An answer, buried deep in a phone, turned the investigation on its head.

They suspected the assailants were Jaipal and Jassi but they had no confirmation.The OCCU team members looked for clues in the abandoned car which had already been searched by the Jagraon cops. The entire state police were on alert. Killing of policemen on duty can't go unpunished. The OCCU team examined everything that they found in the shooters' car. Among the items was a rental agreement for a house in Jagraon, issued in the name of Rajpreet Singh. A police team had already checked the house. No one was there. Only a wooden bed, a small fridge, and two grey plastic chairs next to a grey table had stared back at the raiding police team.

The OCCU team turned its focus on the witnesses of the killing—the cops who accompanied the two ASIs. They had already given their statements. The OCCU team pressed them for more clues, asking them to focus. One of them, homeguard Rajwinder Singh, remembered ASI Bhagwan Singh had taken a photo.

His phone, part of the stuff collected from the crime scene, was searched. It had an important clue—the PAIS on his phone through which he had tried to tally the description of a suspect with Jaipal.

One of the fallen officers had begun a search for gangster Jaipal Bhullar. An OTP notification from the PAIS system confirmed that moments before the shooting, he had been attempting to log in. The system requires an OTP to log the file access record. He had identified Jaipal. And Jaipal had seen him doing so.

Not far from the scene of crime, Jaswinder Kaur, the wife of ASI Bhagwan Singh, felt her chest tighten. Recalling that ill-fated evening to this writer, she said that the previous night she had been restless, weighed down by an unexplainable discomfort. At one moment, she thought she might be having a heart attack. Her husband stayed by her side, comforting her through the night and into the day.

But duty called, as it always does for men in uniform. 'I have to go, but I'll return with your medicines,' he said before leaving around 5.30 p.m. Those were his last words to her. At 6.16 p.m., Jaswinder received the call that shattered her world. Her husband had been shot.

Sitting beside her 13-year-old son, she clutches his hand,

her voice trembling but determined. 'I want my son to join the police,' she says. 'What was Jaipal's enmity with my husband? Jaipal's father is a cop himself. In a way, Jaipal killed his own father that day.'

The ASI's widowed mother (his father had passed away several years ago) now spends her days in silent grief, at times breaking down into uncontrollable sobs. She clings to her memories of how her son meticulously ironed his uniform, polished his shoes, and made his belt buckle gleam. She was proud that her son was a teetotaller—a rare virtue among Punjab's policemen. That pride, now overshadowed by sorrow, transformed each corner of her home into a monument to what she had lost.

◆

Within hours, intelligence units pooled in resources, tracking movements across Punjab. The canter was traced back to Moga, the trail leading to Babbi Baghapurania. Three names emerged—Jaipal, Jassi and Babbi. But the fourth, Darshan Singh, was a ghost. Surveillance watched everything—mobile phones, internet calls, landlines. Then, a sudden lead.

A suspected number linked to Darshan flickered on the grid—alive for seconds in Rajasthan, before disappearing. The OCCU team tore through the highway, whizzing past traffic, pushing through five long hours towards the location. Their urgency was met with humiliation. The Rajasthan Police had unknowingly stumbled upon the fugitives at a chowki, assuming they were petty criminals, mistaking their hardened faces for local smugglers. They had confiscated their vehicle and instead of taking them to a police station in a locked vehicle, the cops asked Jaipal and his aides to walk ahead in handcuffs on the road—a decision that cost them dearly.

Jaipal sensed the weakness instantly. He charged—like lightning, like the animal he had become after years of playing this game. His men followed, disappearing behind him. Then followed three hours of sprinting, clawing through hostile terrain, avoiding highways, dodging rail lines. Jaipal called for help—a coded message through channels he'd established long ago. By the time the police got the scent of it, they had vanished again.

The manhunt exploded in scope. They could be anywhere. Teams chased shadows across Delhi, Haryana, Punjab, Gujarat, and Rajasthan, hoping they'd latch on to a mistake.

28 May

Police then traced them to Gwalior. A hideout was uncovered, but the wanted criminals had already fled. Darshan and Babbi, however, were arrested. Jaipal did not trust anyone—not even his own men. He travelled alone when needed, separating from Babbi and Darshan at Dabra, on the outskirts of Gwalior. During interrogation, Darshan told the police that Jaipal had left in a white Honda Accord for an undisclosed location.

Police teams sifted through toll booth footage in all directions but initially found nothing. A second review, however, flagged a black Hyundai Verna that appeared on several cameras and lingered longer than expected. The vehicle was traced heading towards Varanasi, and intelligence suggested Jaipal was moving in the direction of Kolkata.

It soon became clear that Darshan had misled the police. During interrogation, he claimed Jaipal had escaped in a white Honda Accord, but CCTV footage from the area and the toll plazas showed no such car. The only consistent lead was the black Verna in the background and investigators began to focus on it.

The urgency increased. Kolkata's underworld had a long history of absorbing fugitives.

Then came the break. Using the Verna's registration details, the police traced its owner and address—a location in Panchkula. Local police were alerted. Two days later, the car was spotted parked outside the address.

A routine sweep of the vehicle yielded a crucial clue: a rental agreement for a house in Kolkata. Investigators moved swiftly. The OCCU deployed teams, and the West Bengal Police activated local units.

9 June. Outskirts of Kolkata

The Kolkata Police's Special Task Force (STF) picked up the owner of the flat where the Punjab fugitives were hiding. Jaipal and Jassi were inside when the landlord knocked on the door and asked them to open it.

Jaipal, ever suspicious, cracked open the door. He saw the cops. His eyes met theirs. He shut it immediately. Inside, Jassi reached for his pistol. Outside, the cops already had theirs drawn.

Gunfire shattered the silence. Bullets ripped through the wooden door, puncturing walls and sending splinters and shards of broken glass across the room. Jassi fired back once, hitting an officer in the shoulder. But there was no escape. Jaipal fought, desperate, but his end was near. He crumpled, his body sinking into the debris. In the hours that followed, investigators catalogued the material recovered. Nearly 80 plastic chip cards, each with a different identity; a pen drive filled with Hollywood crime thrillers—material he is believed to have studied carefully.

For years, Jaipal had built his reputation on the ability to vanish. On 9 June, that run came to an end.

The Aftermath

No one from any security agency told Bhupinder Singh about the death of his son. He learnt of it when the neighbhours started trickling in.

Jaipal Bhullar killed was breaking news on all the TV channels and the internet.

Singh collapsed on the floor, unable even to console his wife—Jaipal's mother. Her world shattered. Once a proud mother of two sons and a daughter, she had lost her eldest son while the second, Amritpal Bhullar, was in jail, paying the price for following his brother's footsteps, and carving out a career in crime. They had married off the daughter earlier in faraway Canada.

In the evening, Singh received a call from Kolkata Police asking him to collect his son's body. Crestfallen and helpless, he left for Kolkata, first by car to Delhi and later took a flight.

The body wasn't handed over immediately. 'I was told to check into a hotel booked by the police for us as the body was being "prepared" for the flight back home. I was asked a lot of questions about Jaipal's associates and if any of them was possibly in Kolkata. I was a cop. I knew this was normal but the father in me did not know. I lost patience a number of times and gave way to anger and abuses.'

After two days, the body was handed over to them. Singh had checked into a gurdwara, refusing to accept the police's hospitality. He was followed anywhere he went by three to four SUVs, packed with the STF of Kolkata Police, who had gunned down his son.

'I wanted to see my son's body before it was packed. I gave my statement to Kolkata media, which was camping outside the police station—I suspected foul play. I questioned the Kolkata Police's delay in handing over the body.'

The body was handed over in a coffin, which was loaded onto a plane. The cops escorted them to the plane handing them their luggage and tickets. When they landed in Chandigarh, Punjab Police took over, whisking them into one vehicle, with the body in another.

All this time, Singh just went with what the cops said or did. He would see his son's body only at home. But that was not to happen immediately.

All roads leading to his house were sealed by the police. They did not want a crowd of mourners to gather and cause a law-and-order problem.

When the coffin was finally laid down in the drawing room, Singh collapsed again and cried his heart out holding his wife in arms. His 6'4" son used to run and play in the premises where his lifeless body lay now.

As tears rolled down his cheeks, Singh looked around at the mourners in the house. He recognized many cops in *muftis*, pretending to be mourners to pre-empt any possibility of a problem, mainly delaying the post-mortem. Some of them were already telling him to cremate the body at the earliest. The body though embalmed was still three days old.

Singh had nothing to do with them. Some of the cops were even his friends.

'Out of my house, you all,' he thundered.

And rested only when he had achieved his target. Outside, a DSP of Punjab Police, supervising the road barricades, came to his gate to console and offer advice. Singh let out another volley of abuses at him. He locked the gate and ensured all the cops were out.

Then he went about the task of examining the body and let out a loud scream. 'I saw wounds on the back and arm. These were made by beating. There were marks on the wrist and legs which suggested Jaipal had also been tied. Why were these marks there if he had been killed swiftly in the firing as Kolkata Police claimed?'

He thundered and hurled abuses and announced that his son would not be cremated till a fresh post-mortem was conducted by the doctors in Ferozepore. Now the police and the administration were in a tizzy.

Jassi Kharar had already been cremated.

But another drama unfolded. A woman with a baby in her arms turned up saying she was Jaipal's girlfriend. Jaipal's mother hugged her and kissed the child. She took them to Jaipal's room and asked them to rest there. Singh, still confronting the police and trying to piece together what had happened, was startled. Who was this woman? Was her claim correct? The cop in him overpowered the father and posed a series of questions to the woman. The woman fumbled at many and made good her exit saying she would come back with proof.

Then another came. She had a nine-year-old son. 'This is Jaipal's son,' she claimed before all the mourners. Singh conducted another round of questioning, but this time his wife lost patience with him. 'Leave her alone. I have accepted her,' she roared. The woman stayed with them for a few days even as Singh remained sceptical.

Meanwhile, he did the rounds of the Deputy Commissioner's office, seeking a fresh post-mortem. The DC did not agree but he ordered shifting of Jaipal Bhullar's body to the mortuary freezer as Singh refused to cremate the body.

Singh then approached the Punjab and Haryana High Court, but the court directed him to move the Supreme

Court, noting that the encounter had taken place in West Bengal and therefore lay outside its jurisdiction.

Then he moved the Supreme Court. A helpless father wanted answers to his questions. He was struggling with questions within too. Where had he lacked as a father to have to see this day? Why had he been unable to protect Jaipal and later the younger one from going down this dangerous path to destruction?

As he went from the High Court to the Supreme Court, and back to the High Court, the body lay preserved.

Eventually, 13 days later, the court directed a second post-mortem. The autopsy did not support Bhupinder Singh's accusations of his son being totured. Heartbroken, he resigned and cremated his son.

Another battle at hand had to be taken up. The woman claiming to be Jaipal's wife still stayed with them. Singh with the help of a younger relative lured the kid to a sweet shop and asked about his family. The boy had never met Jaipal but then he had not met his father. There was only one way forward—a DNA test.

The results turned out to be negative. Singh knew he had been right and that the woman's claims had been false. He would never know if the woman just wanted a share in Jaipal's property, or had been planted by someone. Singh lost the will to keep up the fight.

Ever since, his wife, who lost her son, has gone silent and remains indoors, refusing to meet anyone.

Jaipal Bhullar's house in Dasmesh Nagar, Ferozepore, has a stifling atmosphere of despair. A deathly silence blankets the 900 sq. yd plot—a silence so heavy, it seems to have seeped into the cracked walls and peeling paint of the cemented structure. Once a proud home, it now reeks of loneliness and grief, as though the very soul of the house has departed.

Set deep in the rectangular plot, the house stands forlorn as time erodes its once-pristine facade. The driveway, bordered by a lifeless lawn, leads to a structure that has been untouched by a fresh coat of paint for years. The paint on its doors is curled like dried leaves, revealing layers of neglect. Across the lawn, an abandoned cattle enclosure provides a hollow reminder of life that once thrived here, but is now overrun by rust and rot. The upper floor of the house has begun to crumble.

With each step closer, the air feels heavier. This is not a house—it is a mausoleum of memories, where grief fills every nook and cranny, casting long shadows of hopelessness everywhere. The silence is deafening, shattered only by the footsteps shuffling gently through the emptiness, as though even the walls mourn the absence of happier times. Here, time stands still, held hostage by a past too sorrowful to leave behind. That is the story of the houses of the gangsters, when they are no more.

5

Vicky Gounder

A FEW DAYS AFTER SHERA Khuban's death in November 2012, the gang members regrouped for a special ceremony. The venue was a gurdwara. The purpose was to choose a new leader. Jaipal Bhullar was a big name but there was someone bigger—Vicky Gounder.

At 5'9", Vicky—whose parents named him Harjinder Singh—was a muscular youth with a well-knit body, compact and strong.

He was named 'Gounder' by his teachers in the village school.[3] Historically, Gounders were village headmen, landowners, or chieftains—figures of authority and responsibility in rural governance. In some interpretations, the title also connects to the Kshatriya lineage, suggestive of a martial or administrative lineage.

In the Malwa region of Punjab, the term 'Gounder' is often used for someone who enjoys a certain authority around, not to be confused with a bully, who has a commanding presence

---

[3]Gounder is usually used as a traditional title, predominantly in Tamil Nadu, especially among communities like the Kongu Vellalar, Vettuva, Vanniyar, and Vokkaliga. It is believed to have originated from the Tamil word *kaamindan,* which means 'noble protector of the country'. Over time, that evolved into *kavundan* or *gounder*.

and attracts followers. More often than not, such a child or youth is not good in studies and spends more time playing games besides indulging in pranks. Vicky was one such boy.

And 'Vicky' was later added by his 'gangster' friends. 'We fondly called him Vicky Gounder or just Gounder,' revealed Gurpreet Sekhon.

At the investiture ceremony, Vicky was presented with a turban and Shera Khuban's .38 bore pistol. He was anointed leader of the Shera Khuban group.

The group's immediate task was to avenge the murder of the group's founder. On their hit list was Karmiti Sekhon, who already had a long-standing rivalry with Shera Khuban, Vicky Gounder, and Gurpreet Sekhon. Shera had killed a supporter of Karmiti in Piareana village during the 2012 Assembly elections. This election would feature time and again in the stories of the Punjab gangsters. A number of them emerged as gangsters from these elections.

Vicky was the only one to witness the encounter of Shera Khuban. Not the shootout per se, but he was there minutes later as he was scheduled to meet Shera and his girlfriend. He saw the crowd and mingled with it. Later, he would describe the scene to others. He saw Karmiti slapping and pushing around Shera's girlfriend. In a media interview 13 years later, Neeta Deol, one of the gang members, narrated Vicky's description of the post-encounter scene.

Till then, this information or grudge, as the gang members called it, would remain only between them. 'Karmiti wanted to take revenge for the killing of Happy Deora and the murder in Piareana village,' Neeta Deol revealed in the interview.

'See, we killed your Shera Khuban. He talked too much and boasted a lot,' Vicky witnessed Karmiti saying to Shera's girlfriend as Shera lay dead.

Neeta Deol too mentioned this in an interview with journalist Parimder Bariana. (The Punjab Police denies the role of Karmiti Sekhon in the killing of Shera Khuban.)

At the investiture ceremony of the Shera Khuban gang, Vicky vowed to avenge Shera's killing.

He would challenge opponents on the sports field. He would roar while throwing the discus farthest away from his rivals. He would thump his chest on the sports field, though he did not do that on the turbulent Punjab gangland.

◆

Vicky Gounder was born in Sarawan Bodla village, about 26 km from Shera Khuban's village. As mentioned often, most gangsters of Punjab emerged from semi-arid districts like Muktsar, Fazilka, Ferozepore and Bathinda. Top gangsters like Dimpy Chandbhan, Rocky Fazilka, Shera Khuban, Vicky Gounder, Lawrence Bishnoi and Jaipal Bhullar, along with the majority of their supporters or gang members, belonged to these four districts. Far away from the seats of power—Chandigarh in Punjab and New Delhi, the national capital—these districts are surrounded in the east and southeast by Haryana and Rajasthan, while in the west they share the international border with Pakistan. The mighty Sutlej River cuts off this region from the fertile Beas-Sutlej and Beas-Ravi water basins of the Doaba and Majha regions of Punjab.

Due to the international border, life stops at the zero line, as do trade opportunities. The desert winds from Rajasthan make life and agriculture tough. Every year there are protests over shortage of electricity and canal water in these districts. Lack of quality education and healthcare is a perennial problem. To put it briefly, people of this region often complain about how they have been ignored in the march of progress compared to others.

That did not mean that Vicky's parents Mehal Singh and Jaswinder Kaur were dissatisfied with the system and were outlaws, or that their son became a gangster due to the shortcomings of the dusty rural life he was born in.

Instead, Harjinder shared his parents' dream to make a name for himself in the field of sports—a dream once pursued by Shera Khuban and his parents.

Harjinder, nicknamed Jinder by his parents, participated in discus-throw events right from his childhood.

The dusty hard ground he practised on had once echoed with the rhythmic thud of the discus he threw hitting the ground. He won medals, stood on podiums, and basked in fleeting moments of glory.

Seeing potential in him, his father took him to Jalandhar for admission in the Government Senior Secondary State School of Sports there. Jinder was in Class VIII when he started competing at the national level. He won a silver medal in the Under-17 National Championship in Bangalore (2007) and a gold medal in the Under-19 Championship in Hyderabad (2008). He dreamt of participating in the Olympic discus-throw event.

But that was not to be.

Shadows whispered in the background; danger lurked in the form of a wrestler called Thakur—a senior wrestler with a notorious reputation. A dropout wrestler, Thakur got on the wrong side of authority due to his temper and for bullying other youths. Despite being treated as a persona non grata, he continued visiting the sports school, and bullying other youths.

Vicky would have none of it. He wasn't named Gounder—a dominating leader—to cow down before a bully. He took on

Thakur, who retreated but only for a while. He gathered his friends and attacked Vicky and others.

The sports school at Burlton Park was named after Major David Burlton, a British commander who played a crucial role in establishing Jalandhar during colonial rule. Over time, the park became a significant sports venue, hosting international cricket and hockey matches. Later, it also came to be known as Gandhi Stadium and Bishan Singh Bedi Stadium. The AAP leading the Punjab government want the name to be changed now.

A sports event was scheduled shortly and Vicky received information that Thakur and company could attack him or his supporters.

Vicky's gang—Daljeet Bhana, Prem Lahoria, Gurvinder Singh, Ajitpal, and Chhottu—hatched a plan to set things right. Armed with nothing but sheer will, a few *kirpan*s, and hockey sticks, they stood ready to reclaim their pride. When Deepak arrived, flanked by his goons on roaring motorcycles, the atmosphere was fraught with tension. As fists and feet came together, Deepak's goons tasted defeat, and the police came knocking. Charges were levelled against Vicky and his friends under Section 307—the stakes had never been higher.

Another budding sports career was eclipsed. In jail, Vicky met hardened criminals and his group stood together. Soon, they met others like Jaipal Bhullar, Shera Khuban, Sukha Kahlwan, Happy Deora, and Lovely Baba in different prisons. Some bonds turned into lifelong friendships, while others were destroyed due to egos and suspicions. The boy who had once dreamt of sporting triumphs would soon be reduced to a gangster in the eyes of his community, his photograph displayed prominently on crime boards in police stations, instead of occupying pride of place on sports pages.

One such influence was Sukha Kahlwan, a known gangster whose writ ran large in the region at that time. Sukha had links with Vicky's friend Prema Lahoria, through some common friends. Sukha's dominance in the area didn't just mean he could extort money. He called the shots in the underworld to maintain his dominance. One way of doing that was to bring under his wings emerging groups or men like Vicky Gounder.

Sukha intervened in the dispute between Vicky and Thakur (who had links with other gangster groups) and patched up things. Sukha soon left for Australia, while Vicky remained at the Sports School Jalandhar for two-and-a-half years after Class XII.

Vicky grew close to another gangster, Kamaljit Gandhi, bringing him into his orbit. Navdeep Baba alias Lovely Baba of Lidhran was his new confidant, but trouble was to follow. Gurbaj Singh Waja, a member of the block *samiti*, had a long-standing enmity with Kamaljit. One day, after a party, Gurbaj lay in wait for Kamljit, ready to strike. The clash was violent. Another case was registered under Section 307, though initially Vicky wasn't aware of this.

Pressure mounted. Sukha demanded a *rajinama* (compromise), but Lovely refused. Enraged, Sukha had Lovely killed—a brutal betrayal that shattered Vicky, plunging him into unbearable grief. But in his world, grief had no permanent place. Only revenge mattered.

Vicky vowed vengeance. He would kill Sukha Kahlwan.

Vicky and the gang members needed money, so they planned a robbery. Vicky's life then followed the same pattern as that of other gangsters. He lifted cars though he always needed an accomplice. He could never learn how to drive a car. Odd as that may sound, it was true. Later, his associate Neeta would confirm that in statements to the police and the media. Vicky would rob businessmen and snatch weapons. He was an accomplice of Shera Khuban, Jaipal Bhullar and Tirath Dhilwan in several robberies. He also partnered with them in several feuds, fights and gang wars. In Vicky's case, gang wars did not seem to be turf wars or to stamp out another's fiefdom. These were mainly to take revenge for wrongdoings to his 'friends'. This bloodshed over friends, this camaraderie would be a common thread in the life and crime of all gangsters of Punjab.

One of the biggest robberies committed by Vicky was in Amritsar. Sukhvir Singh, a scamster and friend of Vicky's had a unique proposal—to loot aspirants looking for admission in medical colleges under the NRI quota.

They placed a newspaper advertisement offering admission to Sri Guru Ram Das Medical College under the NRI quota.

They were promised seats in exchange for hefty capitation fees—₹45 lakh for admission in the Bachelor of Medicine, Bachelor of Surgery (MBBS), and ₹22.5 lakh in the Bachelor of Dental Science course (BDS). When the aspirants arrived at a restaurant opposite the hospital to finalize the deal, Vicky Gounder, Jaipal Bhullar, Sandeep Bhau, Tirath Dhilwan, and Chandu robbed them at gunpoint and fled with the cash.

Sukhbir Singh was later convicted and sentenced to seven years in prison under multiple IPC sections including Sections 420 and 395. Authorities clarified that the medical college itself was not involved in the scam and had no knowledge of it.

Now they had money. But the gang suffered a jolt as two weeks later, Shera Khuban was killed in a police encounter. The gang members suspected the role of gangsters Lakha Sidhana, Rocky Fazilka and of course Karmiti Sekhon in passing on information to the police.

Vicky led the planning. He already had Sukha Kahlwan on his hit list. The gang learnt that Lakha had hosted a dinner for Shera and his girlfriend a few days before the encounter. They had found something fishy about that. In May 2013, they attacked Lakha in Adampur at a political rally. However, despite being hit multiple times, Lakha survived, though one of his close aides died.

The attack on Lakha catapulted Vicky into big league. The police already wanted him in the Amritsar MBBS seats looting case.

Next was Karmiti Sekhon. The group focused all their energy on him. They followed him around and soon noticed he was living like a king—he was invited as chief guest at several rural functions across Malwa, surrounded by followers and courted by politicians. People approached him to settle disputes in Ferozepore and the adjoining areas, and he even wielded enough influence to affect transfers in the police and administrative departments.

One such event was the rural dog race, a favourite pastime in villages in winter, from December to February. Farmers are relatively free after spending the month of November preparing the fields for the paddy season, and for transplanting the saplings. Known as Rural Olympics, rural games at Kila Raipur in Ludhiana draw people from all over the world. Men pull tractors by their hair or teeth while others display their strength by getting someone to drive a loading tractor over them.

At Khosa Dal Singh village in Ferozepore at one such rural game exclusive for dog's races, Karmiti Sekhon was the chief guest. Several speakers praised his social work and benevolent heart as he often donated money for rural games.

Behind the cheering crowd, Vicky, Jaipal, Ramandeep,

and Tirath sat in a stolen Maruti Swift. Vicky carried a 9mm, Jaipal had a pump-action gun, Ramandeep held a .30 bore weapon, and Tirath a .32 bore pistol. They assessed the crowd, which included at least dozens of armed bodyguards of Karmiti. And Karmiti's followers in the crowd could also turn hostile at them.

But they just had to go in. They had sworn to avenge Shera Khuban's killing. They moved out of the car slowly, weapons hidden in trouser pockets or leather jackets, while Jaipal had his pump action gun inside a *loyi*— a woollen shawl worn by men.

They walked casually but with measured and determined steps, eyes fixed on their target.

Guns spat fire, loud deafening bangs dispersed the crowd, many dogs cowered, and Karmiti Sekhon lay dead along with a supporter.

Vicky and the others sauntered away. No one dared to stop them.

Most of the gang members barring Vicky and Jaipal were caught at different intervals. Vicky and Jaipal stayed separately but both were safe. Since they did not use mobile phones or the internet, they left no digital footprint for the cops to trace them.

Sukha Kahlwan was their next target.

On 20 January 2015, the afternoon sun beat down on GT Road near Phagwara as a Punjab Police van made its way back to Nabha Jail. In it sat Sukha Kahlwan, a gangster whose name struck terror in Punjab's underworld. He had just attended a court hearing and was being transported back to jail under police custody.

As the van approached Paddi Khalsa village, two vehicles suddenly blocked its path. Within seconds, gunmen emerged from the vehicles, their weapons raised. Sukha immediately sensed the danger. According to later media interviews by his associate Gopi, Sukha reached for an assault rifle of one of the policemen, shouting that the men stopping the van had come to kill him. But the policeman refused to hand over the weapon, suspecting that Sukha's friends had planned this ambush to free him from police custody. Sukha had escaped twice earlier. On one occasion, he had scaled the high walls of Ludhiana Central Jail and escaped. On another occasion, he had escaped from police custody after a court appearance.

But no one had killed any gangster in police custody on a busy highway.

Before Sukha could react further, Vicky asked the cops to move out.

He followed the diktat with a barrage of bullets at Kahlwan. More than 30 rounds were fired, ensuring he had no chance of survival. His body slumped, riddled with gunshot wounds, as the attackers continued their assault with ruthless precision.

As Sukha's lifeless body lay in the wreckage, Vicky broke into Bhangra dance, roaring that he had finally avenged the murder of his friend Lovely.

The event established his dominance over Punjab's criminal landscape. The brazen nature of the attack sent shockwaves through the state, leading to immediate disciplinary action against the police officials responsible for Sukha Kahlwan's security. Several officers were suspended or transferred, and an inquiry was initiated into the security lapses that allowed the ambush to happen.

The killing of Sukha Kahlwan remains one of Punjab's most infamous gangland executions, marking a violent chapter in the ongoing turf wars between rival criminal factions.

His death was not just an act of revenge but a message, a declaration in the world of Punjab's gangsters that no betrayal goes unpunished.

Gopi, Sukha's closest associate, would rue in a media interview how he failed to defend his brother. 'I always accompanied him on the court dates. Two cars or jeeps full of our men escorted the police vehicle from the jail to the courtroom and back. We knew he would be attacked. But I had a wedding to attend and Sukha told me not to worry about him. Other guys would be there.'

It turned out that the 'other guys' got stuck in the traffic. The highway which connected Delhi with Jammu via Ambala, Ludhiana and Jalandhar was under expansion. There were diversions on the way. With their meticulous planning, Vicky and associates knew at what point they would strike.

Much later, Gopi would identify all the killers in court; they would be sent to Nabha Jail where once Sukha Kahlwan had been kept. But that would take some time and mark a new chapter in Vicky Gounder's life in crime.

Only eleven months later did the police lay its hands on Vicky Gounder, that too without knowing who they had caught. It so happened that after Sukha Kahlwan's murder, Vicky and the other assailants kept changing their hideouts in Punjab, Himachal Pradesh and New Delhi, besides the Northeast.

Back in Punjab, in November 2015, they lived in Tarn Taran for a while and then at other places. Vicky and Prema Lahoria then visited some religious places and mingled with the crowd. Vicky never carried a phone and like Jaipal, he was very secretive about his hideouts. In December 2015, Vicky, along with Prema and two friends of Prema, went to visit a gurdwara when they were stopped at a police nakka.

Prema and Vicky had pistols and were wary of the police frisking them. When frisking became inevitable, Prema just fled from the scene. But Vicky could not as all the cops had surrounded him. He tried to take out his gun to scare them away but he was overpowered.

The cops did not know who they had caught. Even after a couple of hours in the police lock-up in Patti police station, they failed to realize who the prize catch was. Vicky, like most gangsters, gave fake identities.

It was only when an official from the Punjab Intelligence wing, on a routine visit to the police station, spotted him that he raised an alarm. When confronted, Vicky Gounder is said to have acknowledged with pride. 'Yes, I am Gounder—the killer of Sukha Kahlwan.'

Not long after, he was sent to Nabha Jail, which was meant for dreaded and dangerous gangsters, criminals and terrorists. The jail had maximum security possible and no one could flee. Vicky's associates Neeta Deol, Gurpreet Sekhon and Ramandeep Romi were also jailed there.

An important inmate was Harminder Singh Mintoo, who was facing trial in the 2009 murder case of Rulda Singh, president of the Rashtriya Sikh Sangat, an affiliate of the right-wing Rashtriya Swayamsevak Sangh (RSS). Harminder was the chief of the Khalistan Liberation Force (KLF), a Sikh separatist militant group. Rulda was shot outside his shop in Patiala and later succumbed to his injuries. Investigations linked KLF operatives to the attack.

Harminder was also connected to various other high-profile incidents, such as attacks on Shiv Sena leaders and an attempt on the life of Dera Sacha Sauda chief Gurmeet Ram Rahim Singh. Authorities suspected Pakistan's Inter-Services Intelligence (ISI) of backing his operations.

One of his most notorious acts of daredevilry was in November 2016, when he escaped from Nabha Jail along with five other inmates. Within 24 hours, he was re-arrested in Delhi. But he did not escape alone. Vicky and friends were his partners in crime.

◆

On 27 November 2016, the morning shift at Nabha Jail had begun. Kettles hissed. Radios crackled with dispatch chatter. No one noticed the Mahindra Scorpio until it was too close. It had all the symbols of legitimacy—blue beacon, police plates, men in khaki. It looked like a part of the law. But it brought war.

By 8.10 a.m., all hell broke loose.

Twelve men spilled out from the SUV, rifles barking like wild dogs. The jail gate clanged open and panic overtook the guards. In eight blistering minutes, over 100 rounds lit up the compound. Smoke, screams, the stench of gunpowder—and six ghosts slipped through the breach.

1. Harminder Singh Mintoo, once a quiet boy from Dalli, now the head of KLF, with blood on his hands and ISI on speed dial;
2. Vicky Gounder, a farmer's-son-turned-sharpshooter, trained by bitterness and baptized in revenge;
3. Gurpreet Sekhon, the tactician, obsessed with blueprints, drones, and control;
4. Neeta Deol, quick to smile, quicker to shoot, and sworn to chaos;
5. Amandeep Dhotian, a sledgehammer in a silk glove, with silent musclepower; and
6. Kashmir Singh Galwaddi, a thinker, a smuggler, and a sleeper cell with legs.

Within 48 hours, Delhi Police yanked Harminder off a train at Nizamuddin. He was in disguise, sweating in silence, a duffel bag of secrets at his feet.

Weeks passed. Punjab turned into a war room. Borders were sealed, phones were tapped, and armories inventoried.

Amandeep fell first—picked up in a Ludhiana farmhouse. Then came Neeta, hiding with cousins in Tarn Taran. Gurpreet was arrested a few days later from a house in Dhudike village in Moga. This village has a history. It holds a special place in India's freedom struggle—it is the birthplace of Lala Lajpat Rai,[4] the iconic nationalist and social reformer known as 'Lion of Punjab'.

But Vicky Gounder refused to surrender. He would never be caught alive.

ADGP Jails, Rohit Chaudhary, later submitted a detailed report on how the jail break happened. It spoke of dead cameras, forged IDs, and prison guards asleep at their posts. It said what Punjab already feared: this wasn't just a jailbreak—it was a state-level failure.

◆

Vicky was fond of boasting about his exploits on social media and issuing threats. He openly threatened police officials and, in December 2017, brazenly targeted Captain Amarinder Singh, then Chief Minister of Punjab, in a Facebook post. He soon became an even bigger problem for the police.

---

[4]Born on 28 January 1865, Lajpat Rai's early years in Dhudike shaped his deep connection to grassroots India. Later, the Lala Lajpat Rai Birthplace Memorial Committee was established here in 1956 under the leadership of Lal Bahadur Shastri. The committee built a memorial at his birthplace that was inaugurated in 1965 on his 100th birth anniversary.

In the months that followed, Vicky became a ghost—slipping in and out of hideouts across Uttar Pradesh, Nepal, Punjab, and Delhi. Yet, the whispers never ceased. One tip-off placed him near Sri Ganganagar in Rajasthan. The problem was that no one knew his exact location.

Then came an odd clue. Officers remembered a peculiar detail: Vicky had a fondness for *gulab jamuns*. He was notorious for his sweet tooth, even during his stints in jail. Investigators began combing sweet shops in the area, asking about regular customers. Since the region was sparsely populated, there was only one sweet shop near the suspected hideout.

The shopkeeper revealed that a young man frequently bought gulab jamuns—more often than anyone else—and never bargained. The shop was located near Pakki village. That was the sign the police were waiting for. The shopkeeper identified the customer as Lakha, a lesser-known gang affiliate who lived on the outskirts of town.

The OCCU team—under the leadership of DIG Nilabh Kishore, AIG Gurmeet Chauhan, DSP Bikram Brar, and guided by IG Kunwar Vijay Pratap Singh—moved in. They confirmed the presence of Vicky Gounder and associates holed up in Lakha's house.

On 26 January 2018, the police surrounded the premises. Vicky, along with his aides, Prema and Sukhpreet, exchanged fire with the police for over an hour. When the guns fell silent, Vicky and Prema lay dead. Sukhpreet succumbed to his injuries later.

Not much later, Vicky's father, Mehal Singh, committed suicide. He had been ostracized for the deeds of his son. He had already disowned him, but the ties of the heart never truly snap.

Vicky's killing marked the death of a dream—Mehal Singh's dream of seeing his son win medals on an international platform, perhaps even at the Olympics. Singh would talk about how his Jinder would win the gold medal, the Indian flag would rise, and the national anthem would reverberate across a stadium.

That day never arrived.

Instead, Vicky's father stepped in front of a moving train and ended his life.

6

Gurpreet Sekhon

'WE WEREN'T GANGSTERS. JUST A bunch of friends who zigzagged past the law one time too many,' Gurpreet Singh Sekhon says, as though he is describing a bonfire that got out of hand.

At 6'4", all muscle and stillness, Gurpreet does not need to raise his voice to command a room. But when I ask him what makes a man a gangster, he pauses long enough to make me wonder whether he's calculating the truth or searching for it.

'Courtesy and commitment to friendship—that's all that brought me here,' he says finally. His lips barely part, his voice a low hum—of regret, or perhaps pride; it is difficult to tell.

That commitment cost him dearly.

The police files state it clearly: Category-A Threat. Gurpreet's name is an intrinsic part of Punjab's underworld alongside those of Shera Khuban, Rocky Fazilka, Jaipal Bhullar, and Vicky Gounder. Gurpreet too is a history sheeter.

The daylight killing of Sukha Kahlwan while in police custody; ₹62 lakh looted from Amritsar; a bank hit in Rajasthan; carjackings...the list is endless. And of course, the Nabha jailbreak—a prison escape so audacious, it stunned even the smartest cops.

But here's the paradox—other than firing some shots at gangster Sukha Kahlwan, who had already been hit over ten times by Vicky Gounder, Gurpreet never killed a man.

He is, notably, one of the last men standing. While others died long ago or are languishing behind bars. Gurpreet walks free. No disguises. No safe houses. Just himself, with a salt-and-pepper beard, a neatly tied turban, living in the open in a family set-up that defies conventions: two wives under one roof, four daughters scattering their giggles across a rambling estate in Mudki village in Ferozepore.

When I met him in the summer of 2024, he was freshly out on bail, reclining on a bed like a retired don, nursing old wounds. Nine years behind bars had twisted his back, but not his gaze. A double-barrel shotgun rested beside him like a loyal hound. A beefy guard shadowed the room from one corner, eyes deadpan, fingers twitching.

Beyond the house, Gurpreet's world stretches across 40 acres of green wealth—his family had to sell approximately ten acres just to fund his defence. He runs a marriage palace and a brick kiln—a strange empire for a man whom the state had once called a menace.

'When you're running, you forget who you were before the chase,' he muttered, his voice flat. 'That hour during the 2012 Assembly polls, changed everything.'

Sekhon was referring to the Rahul Gandhi rally in Ferozepore, where he first grew close to Shera Khuban. On polling day, a murder took place in Piareana village. Shera was the shooter. The car he used to flee belonged to Gurpreet. His name did not figure in the FIR, but it surfaced later in the investigation, hovering on the edges.

At the time, Gurpreet Sekhon's dreams had wings—quite literally. He wanted to fly. First as a pilot, then more modestly but still sky-bound, as a flight steward. He enrolled at an aviation training institute in Chandigarh, earning a diploma while walking the glass corridors where young men wore crisply ironed shirts and rehearsed airline smiles.

In between, he had started doing wrestling again. He used to practise and exercise in his village. In Chandigarh's akharas, near the Sukhna Lake, the tall Jat became a favourite—broad-shouldered, polite, with eyes that crinkled when he smiled. He wasn't chasing medals like Shera Khuban or Jaipal Bhullar. It was just for the sweat, the sport, and the brotherhood. Injuries stopped his pursuit to become a wrestler.

◆

After meeting Shera Khuban—and later Vicky Gounder—Gurpreet drifted closer to them. Out of loyalty, out of curiosity, perhaps simply to feel the pull of something larger than himself. He still did not know what Shera had done, or perhaps he refused to believe it. That hesitation would mark the hour that changed everything.

Weeks after the polling-day killing, Shera Khuban arrived at Sekhon's house with his girlfriend, Namjeet.

'We've got married,' Shera said, before asking Gurpreet to drive them to Chandigarh in another car—the police, he feared, might have identified the vehicle he had used earlier.

He did not need to ask for shelter. Shera knew Gurpreet would say yes.

They drove to Chandigarh under a moonless sky, headlights slicing through the dark fields like knives. Gurpreet behind the wheel, Shera in the back, his bride beside him—barely 20, hiding her face behind a scarf. She did not utter a word. Gurpreet did not ask anything.

The rented flat in Sector 15, which Gurpreet kept even though his flight steward dream was over, had seen more weightlifting routines than whispered confessions, but now it had become a hideout, a transit point. Gurpreet handed over the keys to Shera, and left without a word. The next morning, he dropped Shera and his bride to Labour Chowk. He still doesn't know where Shera went after that—or claims not to.

◆

Back in Mudki, life moved on. Wheat ripened. Wrestlers sweated in akharas. No one asked questions. For three months, there was radio silence.

But beneath that silence, something cracked.

Gurpreet's name wasn't in the FIR of Piareana murder, but there were murmurs among Ferozepore Police: 'He was close to Shera. He knows more than he's saying.'

The madness of those days was magnetic, Gurpreet recalls. Back then, a gangster's stardom did not show up on the screen—it was visible on the streets. Men like Dimpy, Shera, Rocky…they weren't just criminals; they were symbols of rebellion, twisted honour, and a daredevil lifestyle. When they walked out of jail, it was like royalty returning home. Villagers lined up for hours. Car processions stretched for kilometres. Dhols pounded. Petals rained. Mothers wept with joy.

No hashtags. No reels. Just raw euphoria in flesh and blood.

Gurpreet remembered being swept up in that tide—not for greed, not for crime, but for *yaari*—friendship. His life did not spiral out of control all at once. It drifted, one decision at a time, each one sealed with the trust of a friend.

And now, long after the guns have cooled, and the names that once dominated Punjab's crime pages are reduced to obituaries or are buried in case files, Gurpreet sits in a quiet Mudki villa with his wives and daughters, repeating his mantra to any reporter willing to listen: 'There's no glory in being a gangster. Only regret...and too many funerals.'

What followed was a haze of hushed meetings and impulsive choices—Gurpreet's descent into crime was marked not only by his proximity to gangsters, but also by his participation in crime. The line between aid and allegiance blurred, and life began to snowball into a disaster the moment he took up the Glock.

Shera trusted him enough to show up unannounced, to bring along men like Ranjit Dupla—later exposed as one of Punjab's most elusive arms smugglers. Ranjit did not speak much, but his eyes bore that cold knowledge of someone whose life had already crossed the point of no return.

It was around mid-August that Shera told Gurpreet about the new hideout—Kamla Nehru Colony, Bathinda. By now, Shera was living openly with his 'wife', as if crime and domesticity could be comfortably packed into one room. The same week, Gurpreet asked for a weapon and a vehicle. Whether it was out of desperation, peer pressure, or the shame of driving nothing while running with the wolves—Gurpreet asked. And Shera delivered.

Soon after came another late-night call, this time to Faridkot. Gurpreet brought along his friend Kulpreet Singh Deol alias Neeta Deol, as he would soon be known—yet another name Punjab Police would come to dread. They drove out to meet Shera and Ranjit, just men on the move. No violence, no plan—but even being in the same room was enough to seal fates.

A few days later, it all cracked open.

Ranjit was arrested in Malout, cornered after a brief

chase. During interrogation, his mouth ran loose. Gurpreet Sekhon's name came up, and with that, began a new chapter of legal doom. The police now had more than rumors—they had reason.

The FIR bore his name—for harbouring criminals. Not attempted murder, not extortion. But enough to get the chains rattling. In Punjab, a land feud might raise fists. But harbouring gangsters? That's an indelible red mark.

From there things spiralled.

One night in Chandigarh—31 August—Gurpreet waited outside a store while his wife shopped in Sector 34. The Toyota Fortuner idled; it was already a target. Three men walked up; no words were exchanged. The gunfire erupted fast and wild. Gurpreet pulled out his weapon and returned fire, his instincts honed in akharas, not in street wars.

No injuries. No arrests. But a message was sent: *We know where you are.*

He suspected the shooters were tied to Karmiti Sekhon, the Akali loyalist who wanted to avenge the poll-day killing in Piareana village. Within minutes, Gurpreet bundled his shaken wife onto a bus at Sector 43. He never said goodbye—just handed her a wad of cash and vanished into the fog.

Bathinda again. That night, dinner was silent and surreal. Shera, still cocky. Lakha Sidhana joined them—a name that once echoed through the crime circles of Punjab. The food was hot, but the room was cold with foreboding.

When Gurpreet returned to Mudki the next day, he stayed indoors.

The breaking news soon came: a shootout; a body in the dust.

Shera Khuban was dead—slain in a police encounter that felt more like an execution. No last words, no second act.

For Gurpreet, the storm had officially landed. His king was gone. His name was now inked in case files. His phone, if he dared use one, was sure to be tapped.

The glamour, the brotherhood, the processions with hundreds of cars—gone in a haze of bullets and betrayal.

For days, Gurpreet stayed holed up in different hideouts in Mudki, mourning Shera. The man who had once sauntered into his life had now vanished—his myth sealed with finality. The grief was personal, but also tactical—Shera's death left Gurpreet exposed. He had already survived a shooting. The streets weren't safe anymore.

In that atmosphere of fear and solitude, Gurpreet reached out—to jail.

It was the first time he spoke to Jaipal Bhullar, patched in through a call with Ranjit, who was already behind bars. Their conversation began with mourning but drifted quickly towards choices. Ranjit urged surrender—live to fight another day. But Jaipal, ever the outlaw, had different plans. He wanted Gurpreet to take a car for a test drive and vanish with it—a clean getaway. He even sent two men to Gurpreet's house for the job.

Gurpreet refused. The urge to reclaim dignity hadn't yet drowned out his inner compass.

But the calm did not last. Under pressure, paranoid and sick from the threat stalking him, Gurpreet made his own move. To send a message, and perhaps regain control, he did what Jaipal had earlier suggested, only in his own time, on his own terms. He called for an Audi test drive. During the spin, he threw chilli powder into the eyes of the company's two associates and disappeared with the vehicle. That was his first solo strike.

In the weeks that followed, his mind fixed obsessively on one name: *Karmiti Sekhon*. The man he blamed, feared, loathed. He stalked the streets of Ferozepore and its outskirts in the stolen car, looking for Karmiti, but Karmiti never showed up.

Until one day in November 2012. Two vehicles, armed and loaded, drove towards Khosa Dal Singh—Karmiti's village. Gurpreet rode with Jaipal and others, all charged with purpose. But fate intervened. Before they could reach the house, Karmiti himself appeared on the road, driving out. The two convoys crossed paths. Gunfire erupted. A blur of bullets. But Karmiti, almost miraculously, escaped unscathed.

After the failed ambush, Gurpreet sank deeper into the underground. He met new names in the nexus: Tirath Dhilwan, Chandu, Jodhan. With Jaipal and Vicky, plans were hatched rapidly—including the hit on Lakha Sidhana. But Gurpreet refused. Lakha was kin, however distant. His conscience—already battered—drew the line.

Lakha, though hit by six bullets, survived.

Then followed more weeks of hiding, shifting locations and slipping through the cracks.

Until November 2013. A familiar address betrayed him—the same Sector 15 flat in Chandigarh that once bred wrestling dreams. The police stormed in. No chase. No drama. Just a quiet arrest that felt inevitable.

By then, his enemies were losing ground. Karmiti Sekhon, his ghost and obsession, was killed by the same network Gurpreet once rode with—Vicky Gounder, Jaipal Bhullar and Tirath Dhilwan. They delivered what he couldn't. And in a way, Karmiti's blood closed the loop.

Gurpreet did not cheer. Instead, he felt the weight shift. Later, arrested in the sensational Sukha Kahlwan murder, Gurpreet was now branded Category-A Threat. He landed in Nabha Jail—more a fortress than a prison.

There, restless and still dreaming of an escape, he flirted with old-school plans—scaling walls, ambushing guards. Then came the blueprint that would make history—the Deodi plan.

He teamed up with Vicky Gounder, Neeta Deol, Khalistani terrorist Harminder Mintoo, Kashmira Singh, and Amandeep Singh Dhotia. The idea was unheard of—walking out through the main gate disguised as authority. From inside, Gurpreet had won over enough jail staff to get his duty assigned near the foyer. From outside, their gang rolled up in fake police gear with forged paperwork, pretending to deliver a criminal to the lock-up.

No alarms. No sirens. Just brazen deception.

On 27 November 2016, as the gates buzzed open, Gurpreet and his crew—Vicky, Neeta, Harminder, Kashmira, and Dhotia—overpowered the guards and joined their comrades in khaki. They drove out of Nabha Jail like ghosts through daylight.

With that began the next chapter—of being fugitives on the road, myths on the move.

The Fallout and the Fadeout

Harminder Mintoo wasn't one of them—not in code, not in loyalty. A Khalistani ideologue, he was the fugitive of another war. So, within hours of fleeing Nabha Jail, the crew did what logic dictated—they separated from him.

Crossing into Haryana through back-channel roads, the group reached Kaithal—but a flashing police barricade made them change course fast. They pulled back, rerouted, and reached Pehowa. That's where they left Harminder and Kashmira behind.

The remaining group moved through Karnal and reached Panipat under cover of night. From there, they splintered. Gurpreet, with Dhotia, Mani, and Rajwinder Singh Sultan, made his way to Delhi and parked their stolen car at a bus stand. Thereafter, they became passengers—no longer drivers of their own fate. They boarded a sleeper coach bus bound for Jaipur.

They did not pause. One city to the next—sleeping on seats, eating on the move, never staying long enough to leave behind footprints. Movement was survival. But beneath the chaos, a plan hummed quietly.

A week later, Jaipur saw a reunion. Gurpreet's entire family—two wives, four daughters, and ageing parents—reached a small hotel. (He was first married to Mandeep Kaur and later to Kuljeet Kaur. He has two daughters each from both. Sekhon doesn't talk about his personal life much.)

For a few precious days, he wasn't a fugitive. He was a husband, a father, a son. The walls of that hotel room witnessed love, exhaustion, and a dream slowly collapsing.

He knew it couldn't last.

Soon Gurpreet moved to Kota, vanishing into the student crowds that filled its hostels and PG rooms. Armed with $1,000 (roughly ₹70,000)—which his family had arranged for him—and street smarts, he embedded himself everywhere like a shadow. Phones were arranged, burner numbers exchanged. Through WhatsApp, he reached out to Ramandeep 'Romi' in Hong Kong, a fixer of fake passports and shady remittances.

Contacts resurfaced—old faces from jail, former associates from a botched Rajasthan bank robbery. A new web was spun.

Gurpreet and his accomplices meandered through parts of North India—from Kota to Jaipur, from Bikaner to Sikar, and into the kind of towns that don't make headlines. A woman named Aman Pannu, originally from Tarn Taran and a mutual friend of Gurpreet and Romi, became a courier of trust and cash. A discreet lifeline, she travelled from Delhi to Jaipur a few times to hand over money.

Eventually, Gurpreet and his family shifted to Indore, renting a flat there. They bought utensils, furniture, made it look like they belonged. They lived that illusion for two months.

In January 2017, there was a call. Vicky Gounder wanted to have a word.

Gurpreet sent his family back to their village. Vicky picked him up at Rattangarh. They drove to Bikaner, then circled back to Indore. The police couldn't track them—partly because Gurpreet's grandfather had filed a harassment petition in the Punjab and Haryana High Court. It granted the family breathing space. But not for long.

Back they went—through the spiral of Rajasthan's towns, eventually landing in Hanumangarh before heading again to Indore.

On 16 January 2017, Gurpreet met Aman again, this time with Raju Sultan. But within days, the news broke—Neeta Deol had been caught. One of their own.

Panic sent them on the move once more—first to Bundi, then to Udaipur. But shadows had begun to creep into every hallway. Gurpreet still hoped for the passport Romi had promised. But the hitch? The passport maker needed Gurpreet, Aman and Dhotia's fingerprints, and they did not trust anyone enough to reveal where they were hiding—not even a fellow criminal.

So they made a fatal decision—to return to Punjab.

In Moga, posing as desperate men in need of cash and weapons, they resumed petty crimes. Snatchings. A vehicle stolen in Ludhiana. Then a Hyundai Verna in Moga.

The police picked up the scent.

On 12 February 2017, they were surrounded. A raid on their hideout in Dhudike village near Moga ended the run. Quiet or loud—we don't know. But the road ended there.

Resurrection and Reflection

On his release in November 2023, Gurpreet Sekhon wasn't the man who had walked into jail after the Dhudike arrest. He came out slower, thinner, with a persistent backache and clipped words. When this writer first met him, his hair was still cropped, his beard trimmed—a first step toward normalcy, but not yet back to the Sikh identity.

By June 2025, something had shifted.

Gurpreet appeared in media interviews, now sporting a long salt-and-pepper beard and a turban, marking his visual reentry into the cultural fabric he had once shed.

'We went to the peak. We were kings,' he said. 'When we called someone, they obeyed. The turning point came when I turned to God's name, reciting the *Guru Granth Sahib*. And, of course, my daughters…and many police officers too, who encouraged me to walk back.'

When asked what the gangster life gave him, he smiled, without warmth.

'Nothing. Just some friends whose word was life and death for me. No riches. No peace. Friends' friends were your friends. Their enemies, your enemies. Forty-eight cases. Some true. Many false. You get stuck.'

And regrets?

A pause, not denial. But a shrug steeped in loyalty.

'I can't call it regret. That would mean standing against what I did for friends. But I'd tell everyone else—don't go down this road. Work. Stay with family.'

And enmities?

The smile faded.

'I don't hold grudges. But people who do…won't forget.'

◆

In December 2025, Sekhon turned over a new leaf and announced his entry into active politics. He fielded 11 candidates—including his two wives—in the Zila Parishad and Panchayat Samiti elections. Six of them, including both his wives, won. Sekhon campaigned aggressively for his candidates, despite opposition from the ruling Aam Aadmi Party.

Days before polling, the police arrested him in connection with an old case. The Punjab and Haryana High Court granted him immediate bail. In subsequent media interviews, Sekhon accused politicians of misusing the police to harass him through false cases.

'For how long will people brand us as gangsters?' he asked in interviews. 'I have completed my sentence. I live peacefully and lawfully, and I want to participate in democratic elections. If people like me support a politician in power, everything is fine. But when we don't, they suddenly remember we are gangsters and send us to jail. How will gangsters ever reform?'

7

Ankit Bhadu

THE EVENING AIR WAS SHARP and clean as the Sector 17 market, Chandigarh, came alive. The smell of roasted peanuts and popcorn wafted through the crowd. January 2019 would end in two days. The winter chill was everywhere, but the market pulsed with a certain warmth—Valentine's Day was approaching, and love was on display everywhere. Red heart-shaped balloons bobbed up and down at shop entries, glowing under streetlights. Discount signs flashed on shop windows. Bouquets, chocolates, perfumes—everything was lined up for the taking.

Couples wove their way through the plaza, hands locked, laughing playfully. Some stopped for ice cream, sharing bites and grins. The cool softy sold in cones by a couple of vendors is a favourite for all seasons. Others lingered at jewellery counters, eyes on rings that hinted at unspoken promises. Newly-weds drifted past, lost in their own world—a private joke, a quiet word—the city of Chandigarh was a blur behind them.

Elders wrapped in shawls walked the same paths, steady and sure. They had built their lives here, chased dreams through these streets. Now they strolled in the dusk, watching the young with a knowing smile. Some carried shopping bags; others thumbed through books. Their presence held the scene together—a reminder of how many stories had started here long ago.

The market was a crossroad. Intellectuals argued over coffee. Professionals strode between stores, eyes on their phones. Dreamers haunted bookstores, fingers tracing titles. Near the plush boutiques, the city's elite swapped quick words. Students and officers moved through the crowd, each caught up in their own mission.

A starry-eyed girl entered a renowned cloth store that sold famous brands in this iconic market. She had just finished a softy cone, which gave a deeper hue to her pink lips. The winter chill had also added a shade of crimson to her pink cheeks. Suddenly, as if reminded of something, she looked back and there he was—in a leather jacket over a white shirt, sky-blue jeans with high ankle Red Tape shoes, trimmed beard. The young man was Ankit Bhadu. He was the life and love of Kanika. The man of her dreams. Only her dreams.

He was also a dreaded gangster. He had blood on his hands. Not just of rival gangsters. But of innocents. The man who lit up her lacklustre life had taken away life from many, destroyed homes, orphaned children, and widowed their mothers.

Ankit did not do this just out of greed for money or to live the good life. Youngsters often struggle with their dreams and ambitions. Some are focused; many are confused and go wherever the tide takes them. The focused ones work to become a civil servant, a corporate boss, a businessman, a singer, an actor, a lawyer, a judge, a politician, among others.

Ankit had none of these dreams. He was not confused either. He had a clear aim. He wanted to be the next Lawrence Bishnoi—the top gangster whose tales he had grown up hearing.

Sherewala, Ankit's village, was just 20 km away from Lawrence's Dutaranwali. The villages not being far from each other only fanned Ankit's dreams.

And achieve his dreams he did, since none other than Lawrence took Ankit under his wings. A few brawls, some extortion calls, beating up rival gangs, taking on the cops, and some murders was all it took. Ankit was the commander of a big area comprising Rajasthan, Punjab and Haryana. He had the guts to command.

Like many others out on a romantic evening stroll without the knowledge of their parents, Kanika too carried a secret. Not just of hiding her relationship with a dangerous criminal from her parents, but something bigger.

She was 'officially' in Canada studying a course in Calgary. Her parents who lived near Abohar had no idea that their daughter had flown back to India on 12 January to be with her boyfriend. They would call her only on WhatsApp thanks to zero charges, and she would talk to them every day—from New Delhi, Shimla, Chandigarh or wherever Ankit took her. A female friend—her bestie and roommate—helped keep the secret. Kanika's parents had spent lakhs on her education and 'bright' future in Canada. Indian girls, especially from Punjab, followed by Kerala, were sought after for nursing jobs in Canada. But here she was with a gangster!

Ankit strolled after her and asked her to buy something for herself. He cared for her. It was not usual for him to roam around openly like this. He was a wanted man. It was not that he was totally carefree. He had his men roaming around keeping an eye on the cops, who could be either in uniform or in mufti. Ankit changed his appearance frequently to remain undetected by the police but that was no guarantee that he would never be recognized. He was not wrong.

Men from OCCU were trying to trace his and his gang members' calls. Ankit did not use the usual phone network but different apps like WhatsApp, Signal and Telegram. The police worked overtime with informers to gather intelligence on his whereabouts, besides looking for his digital footprints. Maybe he would use some of his social media pages someday. The police were also on the lookout for female followers, some of whom could be in touch with him. Maybe one of them could be a girlfriend. If the police could trace her and her phone number, they could locate the gangster.

Kanika wanted to shop for Ankit. She had to fly back on 30 January and wanted to make the most of their penultimate day—29 January—together. In about 24 hours, she would be flying back to Canada.

She had got some clothes for him from Canada. But she wanted to buy more. As she looked for T-shirts and jackets, Ankit strolled towards the shelves displaying Jockey underwears. He picked two—a bright red and a black one, and a packet of socks—grey, white and black.

Little did he know that these undergarments would play a small but decisive role in his doom a few days later.

◆

Around the same time, a man in the Peer Muchalla area of Zirakpur town (a municipal council) in Punjab entered home along with his wife after a long day's work. Peer Muchalla, about 15 km from Sector 17, is one of several villages in and around the Tri-City area of Chandigarh, Mohali and Panchkula which have been gobbled up by rapidly expanding urbanization.

Chandigarh was conceived in the aftermath of India's independence in 1947, when Punjab lost its historic capital,

Lahore, to Pakistan. The need for a new administrative centre led to the selection of a site at the foothills of the Shivalik Range, strategically located between Punjab and Haryana. In 1948, Punjab government formed a committee, chaired by Chief Engineer P.L. Verma, to evaluate potential sites for the state capital. After extensive surveys, Chandigarh was chosen for the centrality of its location, access to water, and favourable terrain.

Over the decades, Chandigarh evolved into a thriving metropolis, influencing urban design across India while maintaining its distinct identity as one of the country's most meticulously planned cities. As it expanded, the demand for more residential and commercial areas surged, necessitating the development of Panchkula and Mohali as satellite towns.

Together, Chandigarh, Panchkula, and Mohali form the Tri-City, a dynamic, interconnected urban cluster.

More than 50 villages, some centuries old, were swallowed up by the massive urbanization in the Tri-City. These villages had history woven into them owing to clashes between Sikh forces, particularly at the time of the tenth Guru, Guru Gobind Singh, and his main general, Baba Bahadur Singh. One finds a large number of gurdwaras in the Tri-City, including Gurdwara Shaheedan. The villages had a sizeable Muslim population too, and some like Peer Muchalla had an ancient connection with Sufi saints called peers. Peer Muchalla, between Chandigarh and Panchkula, came up around the shrine of one such peer, and the village derived its name from him.

Today, however, several tall buildings—residential societies—have come up in the village without any modern town planning. It is common to see a multistoreyed building on a 500 square yards plot.

In one such housing society comprising three floors, lived a couple who were teachers. The building had six flats, two on either side of a stairway. The ground floor meant for parking vehicles was used by the proprietors to run shops, forcing vehicles to be parked along the street.

The couple taught students how to prepare for competitive exams. They lived in a small two-room flat in the building. As they sank into the sofa set, out of sheer fatigue from the day's work and climbing two flights of stairs to their second-floor flat, their younger daughter promptly jumped into the father's lap while the elder daughter, just in Class VI, offered to make them some tea. The couple smiled. They hugged the two daughters and all their fatigue vanished.

In about a week, a little later in the evening, their world would be shaken to the core.

◆

Rajasthan, Haryana, Punjab, and Chandigarh (Union Territory) Police, besides Delhi Police and the central intelligence agencies, were trying to track down Ankit for a reason. His crime sheet says it all.

He had hoodwinked the police so many times that he appeared more a myth—a ghost that terrorized five states.

Ankit, the son of Shiv Parkash Bhadu, clawed his way up from the quiet village of Sherewala, Punjab, into becoming an A-category gangster. Like several other gangsters from Punjab, he too started as a student leader. Ankit's foray into crime though was not accidental. He is said to have picked quarrels with people and got into brawls to attract the attention of Lawrence Bishnoi—Punjab's top gangster.

As Ankit gained attention, he left messages here and there for Lawrence. Lawrence who began his journey by campaigning for candidates of the Student Organisation of Panjab University (SOPU), which he had joined at the behest of leader Vicky Middukhera, always tried to spread the influence of SOPU. Even from jail. He looked for the young and daring, called *sirkaddu* jawans (youths who stand out in a crowd) in Punjabi. Soon Ankit became president of SOPU in Rajasthan.

In no time, his rap sheet became a bloodstained scroll—seven murders in a single year, 27 crimes spread across Punjab, Chandigarh, Rajasthan, Delhi, and Haryana. He was the master of terror—murder, dacoity, kidnapping, carjacking… You name it.

The Gym Execution: Murder of Jordan

In May 2018, Ankit Bhadu murdered Jordan Choudhary, a rival gangster, inside a gym in Sriganganagar. Jordan was exercising when Ankit entered the gym and fired six rounds at him—three at the chest and three at the head. The CCTV footage showed Ankit walking in calmly, shooting Jordan without hesitation, and leaving the scene without panic. The killing was not just a personal attack; it was a public message to rivals and the police alike. Jordan had been active in student politics, and Ankit had warned his associates not to contest the upcoming elections. The murder spread fear among youth groups and consolidated Ankit's reputation of being a ruthless enforcer.

A gym trainer who witnessed the killing said, 'He did not shout. Did not run. Just walked in, shot Jordan like he was swatting a fly, and left. I couldn't move for minutes. I thought I was next.'

The Sadulshahar Escape: Taunting the Police

In August 2018, Ankit escaped from a police operation near Sadulshahar. Acting on a tip-off, the police surrounded a temple where he was believed to be hiding. He had already left, but soon after, he appeared near the barricade, spotted the police, and ran into the nearby fields. During the chase, he fired at officers and then snatched a motorcycle from a passerby to escape. The motorcycle was later found abandoned in Fejerka village near Firozpur.

A police dossier from Rajasthan Anti-Terrorism Squad noted: 'Bhadu escaped despite heavy deployment. Likely aided by local informants. Subject uses multiple SIM cards and travels with armed escorts.'

Ankit's escape embarrassed law enforcement agencies, and showed his ability to move fast while relying on local support.

Training the Next Generation

Ankit recruited young men, mostly college dropouts, and trained them in weapon handling and gang tactics. Videos recovered from his phone later showed him teaching these men how to dismantle pistols, reload quickly, and shoot with precision. He emphasized killing without hesitation and instilled in them loyalty to the Lawrence Bishnoi gang.

One video showed him saying: 'You don't shoot to scare. You shoot to finish. If you hesitate, you die.'

These sessions were not just about skills—they were about building a mindset of aggression and fearlessness.

Extortion, Loot, and Fear

Ankit ran extortion rackets across Punjab, Haryana, and Rajasthan. He targeted gym owners, property dealers, and small business operators. Victims received threat calls and videos of past killings. In Fazilka and Hanumangarh, families fled their homes after receiving threats. The gang often left graffiti or voice notes, claiming responsibility for a crime.

A property dealer from Fazilka said, 'They called at midnight. Said they'd do to me what they did to Jordan. I sold my shop and left town within a week.'

Ankit's extortion strategy relied on fear. One public killing would ensure that dozens paid without resistance.

Just the previous week, Rajasthan Police had placed a bounty of ₹1 lakh on his head. He now carried a total bounty of ₹3 lakh—to be caught alive or dead.

Rajasthan police had a reason. Ankit had mastered the art of escaping, always managing to slip through a small opening in the vast net that the police had cast to catch him. He did that often to Rajasthan, Haryana and Punjab Police.

The last such escape was from Jaipur, the capital of Rajasthan.

The OCCU had received information from Rajasthan Police that Ankit might have moved to Punjab. They named the operation to nab Ankit Operation Pink City, after the 'pink city' of Jaipur.

Ankit did not merely evade law enforcement agencies, he mocked them. He slipped through their nets, vanished after gunfights, and turned his social media into a playground for taunts. One cryptic post, one vanishing act, and his pursuers were left chasing ghosts.

But even shadows leave traces.

Ankit had been careful for years, always slipping through the cracks, always staying one step ahead. His movements were meticulous—no traceable phone numbers, no predictable hideouts, only encrypted messages and international calls routed through VPNs.

But he made a mistake. Love. Add to that his social media pages, some of which he operated himself. That could leave digital footprints which could be tracked down but only after a long and complicated technical forensic analysis of the matter available.

The police had known for a while that Ankit had a girlfriend, though she remained a mystery. No name. No history. No trace. The OCCU team comprised AIGs Sandeep Goel, Gurmeet Singh Chauhan, Gursharan Singh, and DSP Bikram Singh Brar—officers who did not have the word 'impossible' in their vocabulary.

They faced their greatest challenge in Ankit Bhadu and what he was about to do with the Peer Muchalla family—the teacher couple and their two daughters.

◆

For years, Ankit remained a shadow slipping through the cracks of five states, an enigma taunting the police since 2015. Close calls were routine, but in August 2018, the chase turned deadly. Cornered by law enforcement agencies from two states—Rajasthan and Haryana—he made his way through, with bullets shattering the silence of the night, leaving the police scrambling in his wake.

Despite his existence as a fugitive, his voice was never silenced. Lawrence remained his anchor, their conversations held in the digital world, encrypted and untouchable. Multiple Facebook profiles became his megaphone, broadcasting audacious defiance to the world, fuelling his legend.

Tracking him was a nightmare—a ghost without a SIM card, untethered from the conventional digital grid. He moved through cyberspace with precision, relying solely on internet calls and covert messaging. His arsenal of anonymity was extensive—premium VPNs, disposable dongles, and a revolving door of international numbers plucked from illicit apps. Every layer of protection added another wall between him and those hunting for him.

The hunt was relentless. Human intelligence painted half-formed sketches of his hideouts, but the crucial piece remained elusive—technical intelligence. And then came the breakthrough.

The first whisper was vague—a name, a possibility. Ankit Bhadu had a girlfriend, but beyond that, nothing. No identity, no trace, just speculation. Social media became the hunting ground. A girl emerged from the digital haze, her connections suspicious, and her presence too coincidental to ignore. The net tightened. Her Indian records were verified. She was from Punjab but lived abroad—a crucial lead, fragile but promising.

Then came the passport. Immigration pulled out the records, and the puzzle gained shape—she had landed in New Delhi on 12 January 2019. The clock started ticking. Where was she headed? How long would she stay? Every detail of her return journey was perused, dissected for clues.

The search picked up pace. On 24 January 2019, a lookout circular (LOC) was issued. One OCCU operational team was already at Delhi Airport, waiting, watching. Meanwhile, whispers confirmed the most dangerous possibility—she wasn't alone. She was with Ankit. He was here. In India.

Technical intelligence stepped in, mapping her movements. The data trail tracked her shifting location from Yamunanagar, pulling her closer to the NCR region. Another OCCU team was stationed deep in the nerve centre of the city, poised to strike when the moment came.

The noose tightened further. A source delivered fresh intelligence—vehicles. Ankit and his men moved in Toyota Fortuners, Hyundai Cretas, and Hyundai i20s. And then, the breakthrough: a mobile number. It was fleeting, disposable, but it was something. The analysis cut through the layers, tracing it to a dongle, its registration leading straight to an address in Yamunanagar.

Two more OCCU teams moved in. The trap was almost set. Ankit Bhadu was running out of places to hide.

The dongle was a phantom, slipping beyond reach. It wasn't in use at its registered location in Yamunanagar, forcing investigators to mount a relentless 24/7 surveillance operation. Every signal mattered. Every second counted. Then, a sudden blackout—it was switched off precisely at 1 a.m. on 30 January 2019. A calculated move. A deliberate step in the game of cat and mouse.

But the hunt was closing in. By 9.30 a.m., the technical team pinpointed its last-known location—Kundli, near Sonipat—traced to around 7.30 a.m. The investigation closed in further. Toll barriers along NH-1 became critical checkpoints, tracking the ghost's movements through steel and asphalt. At 6 a.m., one of the shortlisted vehicles had whizzed through the Karnal toll, heading towards Delhi. Now the chase had a direction.

Ankit knew the noose was tightening. He played his hand with cunning precision—sending an associate to escort his girlfriend to the airport, a classic misdirection. But the move had been anticipated. The LOC did its job, and at Delhi Airport, she was intercepted, lawfully detained, and placed under a seven-day remand. Her interrogation was inevitable.

Pressure cracked open new paths. Ankit's closest allies surfaced—his contacts mapped, their numbers traced across multiple channels. Then, the unexpected happened. Kanika admitted to shopping with Ankit at Jack & Jones, Sector 17, Chandigarh. The details spilled out, precise and revealing. Surveillance footage was secured. Every purchase, every movement catalogued. The shopping list landed in the hands of the operational teams on the ground—a slim trail through the chaos.

And then, the deeper layers unravelled. Kanika spoke of Ankit's foreign-based associates, the ones who kept him moving, kept him supplied, kept him hidden. Logistics was their lifeblood.

A final lead surfaced—a phone number. It was traced back to a BSNL registration. The location locked onto Sector 22, Chandigarh, on 2 February 2019, a Saturday. But just as swiftly as it was found, it vanished. At 2.30 p.m., it was gone.

The teams remained stationed in Sector 22 for two days, waiting for it to flicker back to life. It never did.

The chase wasn't over, but the ghost had fewer places to run to.

The ghost resurfaced—briefly, fleetingly. Ankit Bhadu's latest digital footprint emerged on 4 February 2019, Monday. His dongle, alive again, pulsed from Peer Muchalla before vanishing into silence the next day at 2.50 p.m. in Sector 34, Chandigarh.

Then, there was movement. The technical analysis painted a picture of his route—on Tuesday, the signal had shifted to Shahbad, Haryana, before doubling back to Chandigarh an hour later. A deliberate manoeuvre, calculated to mislead. But the chase had hardened. Every clue mattered.

Dera Bassi Toll Plaza became the next focal point, scouring records of vehicles that had travelled that precise path from Chandigarh to Shahbad and back. Two leads surfaced—one Hyundai i20, one Mahindra XUV 500. The hunt was narrowing down.

By Wednesday, 6 February 2019, fresh intelligence crackled through the channels. A new number emerged, another trace connecting back to Shahbad the previous day. The cycle continued, moving forward.

Then, on Thursday, 7 February 2019, the dongle flared back to life once more, its location locked—Peer Muchalla. The teams mobilized, closing in on the pulse of the activity. The Mahindra XUV 500, the same one flagged from Tuesday's movement, was found parked outside Mahalaxmi Property Dealer. The building that loomed in front had six flats.

Surveillance intensified. Hours passed. Then, a flicker of a movement—a man stepping out from the third-floor, right-side corner flat. He climbed into the same Mahindra Scorpio, slipping into traffic, heading toward Sector 42, Chandigarh. A team followed, trailing his every turn.

The dongle remained static, its location unchanged. At 6 p.m, the decision was made—no more waiting. The entire Mahalaxmi block was cordoned off. The raid would begin soon. The manhunt was building up to the final act.

◆

Peer Muchalla is a dense urban jungle of stacked housing societies—looming structures rising six storeys and more. The OCCU officers had zeroed in on their target, but the location remained frustratingly imprecise—50 to 100 metres, a narrow radius in a vast vertical maze.

They moved around carefully, dressed in civilian clothes, scanning every detail. No alarms. No sudden movements.

Their confirmation came soon enough.

A Mahindra Scorpio stood parked on a vacant plot. Not just any car—his car. The number plate matched the one they had been tracking. Ankit Bhadu was here. Somewhere in the complex.

But which flat?

The answer came from an unlikely detail: a red Jockey underwear hanging from the railing of a third-floor balcony. A seemingly ordinary object, but one of the officers mentioned Ankit's shopping with his girlfriend. Nearby, other clothes were draped over the railing of the same flat. In any other context, they would have meant nothing. Here, they were enough. The garments matched the ones Ankit had bought recently, which his girlfriend had confirmed during her interrogation. But then, these could have been anyone else's too.

With the dongle location, the suspect Scorpio below, and the garments in the balcony above, the clues seemed to match, the circle tightened. The officers took position, surrounding the building. One team knocked on the door of the third-floor flat.

Gunfire erupted instantly.

Moments earlier, life in this housing society had been painfully ordinary. The housing society was built in a compact, functional style, its flats arranged with tight efficiency. Narrow balconies lined the façade—some facing the street, others overlooking the rear alley.

On the third floor was Ankit's hideout.

On the second floor was the teacher couple's home—a modest two-bedroom flat with a small drawing room at the entrance, an adjoining kitchen, and a corridor leading to two bedrooms. One room faced the street, where the Mahindra

Scorpio stood parked. The other had a rear balcony, leading to a narrow corridor.

The teacher had just arrived home, his youngest daughter skipping beside him, clutching a paper bag from the bakery. Fresh patties. A quiet evening. He eased into his L-shaped sofa, unaware of the danger that was about to crash into his flat.

Then came a violent jolt as the glass shattered, scattering small, ice-like shards across the floor. A shadow moved—Ankit appeared, pistol clenched tight. When the police surrounded his third-floor hideout, he had taken the only route available, climbing down from his balcony to the rear balcony of the teacher's flat on the second floor, where thin, grill-less glass panes offered an easy entry point.

Now inside, he heard the warning from the street below: 'Ankit, you have been surrounded. Surrender.'

The announcment marked the beginning of the standoff. In that charged moment, Ankit lunged. Without hesitation, he grabbed the youngest girl, then the elder one, pulling them in front of him—his shield, his leverage, his escape.

The police on the street fell silent. No sudden moves.

Above, officers were perched on the rooftop. Below, two of Ankit's gang members had already been restrained. But Ankit was still in control.

The setting sun bathed the streets in burnt gold, the shadows deepening with every second. Time was slipping away.

Then, from the staircase, came a flicker of a movement. A commando leapt—silent, swift, unseen.

Ankit did not see it coming.

The commando took a split-second decision. Ankit had a gun aimed at the young girl in his arms. A calculated trigger pull followed.

The bullet cut through the air. A perfect hit. Straight to the head.

Ankit staggered, firing wildly as he fell. Bullets tore through the room, into the walls, into the floor. Splinters sliced into the girls' legs. A cop took a hit.

But the police achieved its objective. Ankit Bhadu lay dead. The girls were saved.

8

Teja Mehandpuria

IT WAS EARLY JUNE 2020. ACP Girish Kumar (name changed on request) stepped into the Mataur police station lock-up in Mohali, black jogging suit sticking to his back, sweat still drying from the morning's drill. He did not expect the man on the floor, Teja Mehandpuria, to look like he'd just walked out of a magazine ad—branded black T-shirt, Levi's jeans, tan leather belt with a cheetah buckle.

Even with his hands tied behind his back, Teja's shoulders looked like they could snap the ropes. With spiked hair, he wore a winsome smile under a thick, trimmed beard.

'Sir, you really need new shoes,' Teja spoke first, grinning as his eyes dropped to the ACP's feet.

ACP Kumar looked down at his battered Adidas trainers. He'd worn them since the police academy days. Though he passed out two years ago, the shoes held a sentimental meaning for him. He wore them on every morning PT drill, wearing them down a little more each time.

Worse still, his huge St Bernard had merrily chewed on these the night before.

Teja's own shoes—brand new Nike reds—stood out.

ACP Kumar ignored the jab. 'I'm ACP Girish Kumar from Ludhiana. You know why I'm here?'

'I guess so,' Teja replied, still smiling.

'So, where's the gold jewellery? And the diamonds?' ACP Kumar kept his tone light.

Teja's eyes narrowed. 'You know I've been here since last night. These guys tried hard to question me. No one gets anything out of me.'

ACP Kumar nodded at Teja. 'Doesn't look like they tried very hard.'

Teja laughed, sharp and sudden. 'No one dares. I'm Teja Mehandpuria. They have families. They know what I can do once I'm out.'

'Sure. But sometimes a cop is as mad as you.'

Teja stared back, silent. Then smiled and said, 'Let me gift you a pair of new jogging shoes. Yours are too ordinary.'

ACP Kumar let out a laugh, then waved at a constable. 'Get him a Coke.'

Teja drained the bottle in one go and burped. 'I like you, Sir. I need to make a phone call.'

ACP Kumar nodded and handed Teja his phone. 'Put it on speaker.'

Teja agreed. The constable untied his hands. Teja dialled a number. No answer. He texted, then tried calling again.

A girl's voice responded, breathless. 'O my shona, my babu, where are you? I haven't eaten since last night. Whose number is this?'

'I'm okay. Don't worry, baby,' Teja said reassuringly.

'Oh, I'm so happy. I am dancing. You are alright. I was on the verge of dying.'

Teja chuckled. 'Listen, I'm with a nice police officer. We have to return the jewellery.'

'Noooo,' she wailed.

'Yes, baby.'

◆

The jewellery he was referring to was from V.K. Jewellers, a shop in Ludhiana.

On a wintery 29 January 2020, at 2.30 p.m., Teja, dressed in jeans and a black bomber jacket with a fur collar, walked in with three friends—Sam, Preet, Bhushan. The shop was empty except for a helper. Vinay Jain, the owner, had just stepped out for pencil cells for his daughter's TV remote. When he returned, four men were inside, talking to the helper.

Jain felt a chill. He was more of a wholesale jeweller. These four men did not look like jewellers. He had never seen them earlier. *Maybe they were new customers*, he thought and stepped inside the shop.

Immediately Teja swooped in. Jain felt the cold steel pressed to his head. Over the next 15 minutes, he remained frozen, not knowing what was happening. In two days' time, he was to fly to the US for a two-week holiday, and to attend a relative's wedding in California.

Teja and his gang decamped with 2.1 kg of gold, some necklaces, silver bowls, coins, stones, and even diamonds. The loot was worth more than ₹2 crore.

◆

ACP Kumar waited as Teja and his girlfriend talked. Then Teja returned the phone, telling him where and when to pick the jewellery. 'But promise me, no harm should come to Roopam,' he implored, the look in his eyes more a warning than a plea.

That evening, Roopam arrived on her TVS scooter, with another girl riding pillion, at the designated spot. She did not stop. Just tossed a small bag on the roadside near Nawanshahr, about 20 km from Teja's village Mehandpur. It had already been decided that the police wouldn't arrest her.

Roopam wasn't Teja's only girlfriend. There was Prema in Delhi too. Neither knew about the other, but the police would find out soon.

Roopam had fallen for Teja long ago, even before she had met him in person. She lived a few villages away from Teja's village. A Class XII student, she cycled to school with friends, scared of the boys who would circle and jeer at them on their motorcycles. One day, four boys blocked their path. Roopam's bold friend bluffed, 'Get away. Teja Mehandpuria is my aunt's son.' The boys sped off. Roopam's heart pounded at the name. She searched for Teja online, and kept revisiting his Facebook page, and other pages made by his 'fans'. She liked some of his pics.

That was five years ago. When she dropped a message, they began chatting. She had no idea if Teja was messaging as a free man or was in hiding or in jail. Teja never told her about his location. But she felt his eyes following her wherever she went. She was scared but she felt secure too. No one approached her anymore with evil intentions. No one harassed her anymore.

Shortly, they started meeting. And she learnt everything about him.

Teja was the youngest of three brothers. His father died when he was still a child. The father was an Amritdhari Sikh, as was his mother. She asked her sons to recite verses from the *Guru Granth Sahib* everyday. Teja was the most devoted. Everyday, he would recite the verses at his mother's feet. She dreamt that he would become a priest. While studying under a village *granthi*,[5] Teja met Giani Bhagwan Singh Bhindrawale,

[5]A Sikh religious officiant responsible for reading and maintaining the *Guru Granth Sahib*, and for conducting daily prayers and related duties in a gurdwara.

and joined the Dam-Dami Taksal at Mehta Chowk, Amritsar. After two years of the scriptures, discipline, and faith, when he returned home in 2009, he had the aura of a youth on a spiritual path.

Then, everything changed one day. Barely 16, Teja observed his silent mother often returned disturbed from their small field measuring barely an acre and a half. Mehandpur, a developed village, boasted of concrete roads and cemented houses. Many people from Mehandpur had gone abroad, to the West, and sent bountiful riches back home. The village already had rich farmers, thanks to their large landholdings and plentiful crop from the land nurtured by rains, and rivulets bringing fertile sand and minerals from the foothills of the Shivalik Range. But Teja's family had lost their breadwinner early and half of the original three acres to relatives—after his father's death, his grandparents and his mother went separate ways.

Teja sensed something was wrong. He asked his brothers if they knew anything. They had no idea. So, one day, along with his immediate elder brother, Jaswinder Jindi, he followed his mother. They were shocked to see their neighbour following his mother. She kept evading him, and warned him to mend his ways.

The next day, the neighbour did the same thing. That was enough for Teja. He waited for the man at an isolated place with his brother. He asked the man to stop harassing his mother. Instead, the neighbour abused him. That was it. Teja pounced on him using all the strength and strangled him with a *parna*—a small turban cloth. The man was twice his size. Teja's hands were stronger. His rage had built up to a storm.

Along with his brother, Teja landed in Ludhiana's Borstal Jail, and cut his hair and beard—he left his old self behind. He told his mother not to visit him: 'I can't see you sobbing.

I'm happy with what I did.' In jail, his notoriety grew. He met hardened criminals, and built his network.

Seven months later, starting with Teja's bail in the case, life became a vicious circle. Thereafter, he would be in and out of jail, pursuing a life in crime, making rivals, earning notoriety, besides always being on the radar of the police. He wanted to live the good life too. Branded clothes, luxury but stolen cars. Swanky hotels, and then in hiding in dodgy, unliveable places. For days on end, he would stay at the motor houses[6] of his friends in several villages.

To keep up the lifestyle, pay lawyers, bribe cops, Teja needed money. Robberies became routine. The Ludhiana heist was just one among many. Several others had taken place earlier.

On being granted bail after his first murder, Teja returned to his village as a man feared by one and all. He got into more fights. Sometimes, over personal issues, and often over matters related to 'friends' who he was loyal to. He also intervened in property disputes.

A few months later, Teja's friend Pali sought his help in a property dispute with a man nicknamed 'Shraabi' who was notorious as a local muscleman. Teja beat him up—his way of settling the dispute and forced the man into submission. Following the police case after that, he took shelter in the motor house of his friends—Chota Thakur and Wada Thakur (younger and elder Thakur), two brothers from Balachaur. Eventually, owing to police raids, he surrendered.

---

[6]'Motor house' in Punjab is a small brick room built next to a tubewell in the fields—a place for farmers or labourers to take short breaks. Since these are far from the villages and lie hidden among fields, they make convenient hideouts.

Out on bail, the Thakur brothers needed to settle an old enmity with someone. Teja did the job using sharp-edged weapons and landed in jail again.

A few weeks after his bail, Teja took recourse to violence again to settle another property dispute of his relatives. Over time, his rivalries grew bitter and some rival local gangs began targetting his friends. A rival gang beat up his friend Fauji, and made an obscene video. Teja beat them to pulp. When a hospital manager harassed his cousin, Teja 'settled' it his way.

In between, he robbed some people and lifted cars too. While on the run after the Ludhiana jewellery robbery, Teja stole a Maruti Swift car from Mohali and snatched a weapon from a police officer. It was after a string of such crimes that he came under the radar of a specialized unit—the OCCU of Punjab Police, later rechristened the Anti-Gangster Task Force (AGTF). This group of decorated cops, whose mission was to end the menace of gangsterism in Punjab, pursued him relentlessly. It was this OCCU team which tracked him down and arrested him. It was in their custody that ACP Girish Kumar first met Teja Mehandpuria.

◆

In June 2022, ACP Kumar—now the SP—met Teja again, this time in Bathinda's high-security jail. Teja wore a simple kurta-pyjama, a *kesri patka*,[7] and a flowing beard. He had become an Amritdhari Sikh.

SP Kumar greeted him. 'Welcome, Teja. Good to see you. You've changed your appearance.'

---

[7]A saffron headcloth worn by Sikh boys and young men; a simpler form of the turban.

Teja stood by the wall, legs locked. 'I won't sit on the floor. Not anymore.'

SP Kumar smiled. 'I'll stand too.'

Teja laughed. 'You're polite, Sir. I'll sit, but make sure no one comes in. I have an image to keep. But you—your good nature can floor anyone.'

SP Kumar nodded. 'You know Moosewala has been murdered. Any idea?'

Teja's eyes hardened. 'I don't snitch. But the buzz is Moosewala was killed for his fame; killing him would make the killers the king of the Punjab underworld.'

SP Kumar switched the topic. 'You've changed. Why?'

'I did a lot for myself. Now I want to do something for the *qaum*—the Sikh community.'

Teja had come in contact with men from Harvinder Singh Rinda's outfit, Babbar Khalsa International, which was operating from Pakistan.

SP Kumar pressed on. 'What have you gained from all this? The law can't protect the innocent?'

Teja's voice was steady. 'The jails are full of so-called gangsters like me, but we're only responsible for a fraction of the cases. The police keep us entangled in false charges. The innocent die every day. When evil raises its head, someone has to pick up weapons.'

SP Kumar nodded. 'Thank you. And for your cooperation in the jewellery case. That was my first big challenge.'

Teja grinned. 'Your politeness did the trick, Sir.' He paused. Then Teja looked SP Kumar in the eye. 'You are not like the others. You ask, you listen. Maybe that's why people talk to you.'

SP Kumar shrugged. 'I just do my job. Sometimes, that means talking. Sometimes it means running in old shoes.'

Teja laughed, his laughter echoing in the bare room. 'Next time, I'll get you a new pair.'

SP Kumar smiled, but his eyes were serious. 'Do you ever think of what your mother wanted for you?'

Teja's jaw tightened. 'Every night. But you can't go back, Sir. Not when your community needs you.'

SP Kumar stood firm, and offered his hand. 'You can always change direction. Even now.'

Teja looked at the hand, then shook it firmly. 'Maybe. But not today.'

The warden led Teja away. SP Kumar watched him go, the orange light from the corridor flickering across Teja's back.

Outside, SP Kumar paused in the empty corridor. The air smelled of sweat and disinfectant. He thought of the gold, the guns, the lives twisted by violence and fear. He thought of Roopam, waiting by a silent phone, and of Teja's mother, praying in a village house split by old feuds, and missing her three sons—two in jail and the third one, who she had managed to send abroad before he too was sucked into the same hell.

◆

A dossier on Teja Mehandpuria based on his interrogation, and investigations, besides the interrogation of his co-accused, accomplices, sympathizers and intelligence inputs by OCCU (AGTF), provides insights into how he turned from a gangster into a radical.

Teja was incarcerated in several jails, and each stint helped him learn something new—from building up a gang network to terrorism. His journey into the dark world of radicalization began within the cold, unforgiving walls of Patiala Jail after the Ludhiana jewellery robbery. Initially, Teja was just another inmate, clean-shaven and unremarkable. But his life took a dramatic turn when he crossed paths with a prominent Sikh prisoner who was a convict for the assassination of a top political leader. He asked Teja to return to his moorings where he could commit himself to serve the community. Teja became an Amritdhari Sikh again. But he did not follow the path of spirituality. Instead, he persisted with the gangster's way, adding radicalism to it. Now, he talked about avenging the wrong-doings to the Sikh Panth. He mentioned Operation Blue Star (1–10 June 1984) when the Indian Army stormed the Golden Temple. He talked about the 1984 anti-Sikh riots. He talked about three rape cases in Nawanshahr and Balachaur.

While in another jail, Teja got in touch with Dharminder Singh Gugni, a radicalized gangster. Dharminder is associated with the Kala Hawas gang. He has been involved in multiple criminal activities, including the murder of the Congress sarpanch Rajwinder Singh Grewal, also known as Ravi Khwajke. Dharminder reportedly feared that Khwajke would kill him, leading him to hire Davinder Shooter and his gang to carry out the assassination.

Then, Dharminder introduced Teja to Jagtar Singh Hawara, a key figure in Punjab's terrorism and the state's subsequent years.

Jagtar was a high-ranking member of Babbar Khalsa International. He was convicted as a key conspirator in the assassination of Punjab's 12th Chief Minister, Beant Singh, in 1995. The assassination was carried out by Dilawar Singh Babbar, who acted as a human bomb, killing Beant Singh and several others.

Jagtar gained further notoriety when he escaped from Burail Jail in 2004 by digging a 90-foot tunnel with his bare hands, only to be recaptured in Delhi in 2005. He was sentenced to death in 2007, but later the Punjab and Haryana High Court commuted his sentence to life imprisonment. He is currently serving his sentence at Tihar Jail in New Delhi.

In 2015, a *Sarbat Khalsa* (congregation of Sikhs) declared Jagtar Singh Hawara the *Jathedar* (leader) of the Akal Takht, the highest seat of earthly authority of the Khalsa, though this declaration remains disputed and unrecognized by the Shiromani Gurdwara Parbandhak Committee (SGPC).

Jagtar's ideology and actions, further reinforced Teja's radical beliefs.

With Teja's connections expanding, his network now extended beyond the prison walls. A Khalistani activist from the US—a mutual friend of Jagtar and Dharminder on Facebook—frequently provoked Teja against some Hindu leaders suspected of orchestrating certain sacrilegious incidents in Punjab.

In June 2015, torn pages of the *Guru Granth Sahib* were found in Bargari, Faridkot District, leading to massive protests across Punjab. On 14 October 2015, the police fired at demonstrators in Kotkapura and Behbal Kalan, killing two people. Several other incidences of desecration were reported in different locations like Mishriwala, Bath, Kohrian, and Sarai Naga between 2015 and 2021. These had a far-reaching impact on the social, religious and political landscape of Punjab, directly causing the downfall of the Akalis and the rise of the AAP and a number of gangsters and radicals.

Much later, the police would find a chat on Teja's phone that revealed discussions with a Khalistani activist from the US about avenging Ghalu Ghara (Operation Blue Star). These digital exchanges seemed to have fuelled Teja's anger and determination, pushing him further down the path of radicalization.

He had come in touch with Khalistani activists earlier too but had not become radicalized immediately. During his time in Nabha Jail in 2015–16, Teja formed a close bond with another Khalistani activist Harminder Singh Mintoo. Harminder would remain the kingpin of several high-profile crimes in Punjab, including the murder of Rulda Singh.

Harminder was later involved in the Nabha jailbreak. Nabha in Patiala District was a maximum-security jail. That is till Harminder Singh Mintoo along with gangster Gurpreet Sekhon and four others pulled off the daring Nabha jailbreak on 27 November 2016. A group of gangsters and militants, dressed as police officers, stormed the prison and opened fire on security personnel, allowing six prisoners to escape. Teja had been shifted to Kapurthala Jail before the jailbreak.

Harminder was the mastermind behind radicalizing youngsters, brainwashing them into dedicating their lives to the cause, planning operations, and constantly changing their appearances. Their discussions about a Sikh separatist movement were intense and frequent. Harminder's guidance and encouragement strengthened Teja's resolve to act.

In Kapurthala Jail, Teja met Billa, another gangster-turned-radical. He promised to deliver weapons to Teja for action against the Hindu leaders and others accused of sacrilege.

In 2019, Teja met Rachhpal Singh Daula, an ally with similar Khalistani ideology. Rachhpal's connections with cross-border drug smugglers provided Teja with weapons and hideouts. Despite Rachhpal absconding in a murder case, he continued to support Teja's demands fully. They had plans to carry out strikes on Hindu leaders and others accused of sacrilege.

When the OCCU team caught Teja in June 2020 for a carjacking in Mohali and the Ludhiana jewellery robbery, the police recovered several fake identity cards including driving licences and Aadhaar cards. They also recovered police uniforms that revealed Teja's plan to masquerade as a cop to get as close as possible to his targets.

After spending over two years in Bathinda Jail, Teja was released in November 2022. Besides regrouping with his gangster network and radical underground workers, Teja met Roopam again.

They kept changing places, from the meadows and icy peaks of Himachal Pradesh to Uttarakhand, then New Delhi and several metros.

But Teja had some tasks at hand. He was committed to radical leaders who had given him the tasks to attack right-wing leaders, police installations and offices of Hindu organizations. He pushed his gang members to arrange for weapons and do a recce.

On the night of 8 January 2023, things were calm inside Phagwara City Police Station, where SHO Amandeep Nahar sat down for dinner with his team. Among them was Constable Kamal Bajwa, not just a gunman but a family figure. Nahar's five-year-old daughter called him 'Kamal Chachu', running to greet him even before her own father returned home. Bajwa would play with her for a few minutes—a brief moment of warmth—before duty pulled him back to his own house.

The wireless crackled to life—a Hyundai Creta had been carjacked at gunpoint by four men in their jurisdiction. Immediately, the dinner plates were abandoned, chairs scraped against the floor, and within seconds, the team was racing towards their police jeep. A bank employee, the victim of the robbery, had GPS tracking in his car, and shared the live location with Nahar.

The gangsters had made a tactical move, avoiding the Delhi-Amritsar highway and its offshoots leading to Pathankot and Jammu. Instead, they took a rural road running parallel to a canal, hoping to evade pursuit. But fate had other plans.

The police closed in fast. A fallen tree blocked the gangsters' path, forcing them to stop and turn back. There was no escape. Then, gunfire erupted. Bullets tore through the night. Constable Bajwa was hit and went down as his team retaliated. Three gangsters were wounded, later identified as Ranjeet Singh alias Jeeta, Vishal Soni, and Kulwinder Singh alias Kinda. But Yuvraj Singh alias Yora, the most ruthless among them, escaped into the darkness.

With red alerts sounded, the AGTF launched a relentless pursuit. Days later, intelligence led them to a hotel in Zirakpur, near Chandigarh. Yora had checked in under a fake identity, believing he had outrun the law. As the police stormed the hotel, Yora opened fire, forcing a brief but fierce encounter. There was no dramatic escape this time—he was injured and arrested, putting an end to his short-lived freedom.

One of the phones the police tracked down belonged to Roopam. It was a careless slip—she was deeply involved with Teja, and that connection would soon lead to his undoing. When the police raided a hideout, they found Roopam—but Teja escaped once again. That's when he snapped.

For the first time, Teja was truly afraid—not of the police, not of death, but of losing Roopam. He made phone calls to the police, issued threats laced with fury, if any harm was done to the love of his life. He promised bloodshed if Roopam wasn't released. He was reckless, blinded by rage. But in his desperation, he exposed his location.

The AGTF team had been waiting. On 25 May, near Bassi Pathana, Teja was surrounded. Led by DSP Bikram Brar, AIG

Sandeep Goel, DSP Gursharan Singh, and their team, the police closed in.

Teja refused to surrender. The air exploded with the exchange of gunfire, each bullet stripping him of his imagined invincibility. And then there was silence. Teja was dead.

Roopam was left behind, alive but alone, staring at the man who had fought the world for her—and lost.

9

Davinder Bambiha

GANGSTERS GAMBLE WITH BULLETS, TRADE in blood, and thrive on three fragile currencies—name, fame and fear. For most, the story ends as soon as their pyre cools—their voices silenced, their terror transforming into memory, and their names becoming mere footnotes in police files.

But sometimes, a man dies and refuses to stay 'dead'. His shadow stretches across villages, and his dubious fame grows even larger in death than in life. His gang multiplies. His enemies multiply faster. The fear he planted in men's hearts blooms long after he is gone.

This is the story of Bambiha—the Sultan of Faridkot, the outlaw who wouldn't die.

Davinder Singh Sidhu—the name emerged from a dusty village on the Moga-Faridkot border and resounded through the gunfire of a hundred feuds. The world would call him Davinder Bambiha. To the police, he was a fugitive. To his rivals, he was their nemesis. To his followers, he was not merely a gangster. For them, the Sultan Bambiha Gang was a badge of honour.

This is the story of a boy who entered jail weeping, terrified of the night, and walked out a warlord; the story of a young kabaddi player whose grip on men became a grip on Punjab's underworld; the story of a name that outlived bullets, betrayal, even death itself.

Davinder's story echoed not only in the streets of Punjab, but across social media, in policemen's chargesheets, and through the whispered fear of rivals. His gang wasn't just another entry in Punjab's long list of criminal outfits. It became the fiercest rival to the vast Lawrence Bishnoi Syndicate, fuelling a feud that continues to stain Punjab's soil red. The gang operates even today.

This clash of titans birthed murders too frequent to count. Police records connect the rivalry to at least 20 killings across Punjab—people killed either in marketplaces, weddings, or during drive-by shootings or ambushes on highways. Some were gang members; others, high-profile figures. The most infamous killing was the broad daylight assassination of singer Sidhu Moosewala near his village Moosa on 29 May 2023—a killing that shook not only Punjab but the entire nation. Before him, this enmity had consumed Vicky Middukhera, an Akali youth leader and rising politician, who was shot dead in Mohali on 7 August 2021. In between came the murder of kabaddi player Sandeep Nangal Ambian in the middle of a kabaddi field, and, earlier still was the killing of Ravi Khwajke, a young Congress leader close to anti-Bambiha gangs.

Each killing etched bloody lines across the map of Punjab. And at the heart of them all lay the shadow of a boy—Davinder Singh Sidhu—from a small but significant village—Bambiha Bhai—in Moga District. Locals insist it was first called Bambiwala Bhai village, after a bird—the Bambiha, or pied cuckoo, also known as the *papiha*—whose cries linger in the Punjabi imagination. Founded in the 1700s, Bambiha Bhai carries pride, reverence, and rebellion in its soil.

Mai Umraai, wife of Bhai Bhoom Chand, a descendant of Bhai Bahilo Ji, the devout follower of Guru Arjan Dev Ji, is said to have founded Bambiha Bhai. Mai Umraai is remembered as one of the few women to establish a village in recorded history. While returning from Alisher in Mansa with her family, she halted at a pond. There, in the humid dawn, a Bambiha bird cried. She took it as a sign, naming the outpost Bambiwala Toba, which would later be called Bambiwala Bhai, and with time, be renamed Bambiha Bhai.

Besides being fertile, the land became known for its scholars, patriots, and emigrants. Poet Babu Rajab Ali once called it 'the cradle of knowledge, where one sits among the wise.' Its diaspora now stretches across Canada, the US, and Europe. Many of its sons serve in the Indian Army. But the headlines chose to immortalize a son called Davinder Singh 'Bambiha.'

Davinder was born into a family neither poor nor deprived of tradition. His father, Iqbal Singh, was a respected schoolteacher, and also a kabaddi player admired at local tournaments. Tragedy struck early—when Davinder was just four, Iqbal Singh suddenly died of a heart attack, and the household lost its anchor. Raised by his widowed mother, Paramjit Kaur, alongside two older sisters, Davinder grew quiet, shy, and introverted, restrained by circumstances. The family owned seven acres of land.

On the kabaddi field, however, Davinder became something else. Athletic but not bulky, graceful yet not intimidating, he was swifter than most, his wiry frame deceptive. As a raider, he would slip past tackles. As a defender, he locked onto opponents like iron until they fell gasping in the dust.

'When he held a raider,' recalls his mother, 'he wouldn't let go. He wasn't built big, but his grip was like steel.' His mother now lives in a modern house that stands across a vast courtyard in the village, where concrete streets, numbered much like an urban colony, have replaced mud houses.

Davinder completed a course in welding from the Industrial Training Institute (ITI), Faridkot. 'He got good marks and was offered a job. His teacher once told me my son was skilful with iron. I did not know my son would use that expertise to handle weapons, even cleaning some rusty ones, to shoot at will—precise, deadly, and always on target,' continues his mother.

Then misfortune struck on 23 November 2010.

That Monday, Amrik Singh—a neighbour and childhood friend embittered by betrayal—came to Davinder's house. Amrik had once loved a girl in college, but lost her to Harpreet Singh, a friend from Jeoonwala village. Love turned into rivalry; jealousy sharpened into rage.

That evening, Amrik convinced Davinder to ride with him on his new motorcycle. Their route wound toward Samalsar, where Amrik planned to 'talk' to Harpreet, who was often seen in the company of the girl after the breakup. Davinder agreed. After all, it was supposed to be just words.

The encounter ended with anything but words.

On the village outskirts, they saw Harpreet walking with his friend Navdeep. Amrik and Harpreet had an argument. Then, Amrik pulled out his father's stolen pistol.

Shots shattered the quiet. Birds scattered from the trees. Harpreet collapsed, and died gasping. Navdeep slumped beside him, blood pouring into the dirt.

Davinder stood frozen until Amrik yanked him away, and they fled. Navdeep, half-conscious, managed to call his family. Relatives rushed the victims to Kotkapura hospital. Harpreet was declared brought dead. Navdeep survived long enough to name his attackers.

Within hours, their names circulated. Murder charges followed. Amrik surrendered after few days; Davinder did not. For weeks, he hid among relatives, terrified of the lock-ups he'd only heard about—sodomy, torture, men turned into insects. But nobody can run forever.

Police interrogated his kin; they dragged neighbours out for questioning. His mother remembers: 'He kept telling me, he did not pull the trigger. He just went along. But who would believe him? And the longer he stayed away, the stronger the suspicions grew. At last he had to surrender.'

He was no longer *the* kabaddi boy of Bambiha Bhai. He was now Davinder Singh Sidhu—an undertrial for murder.

The gates of Ferozepore Jail slammed shut behind him. His descent into hell began.

Constables taunted: '*Nava maal aa gaya. Eh vi kehnda hai nirdosh hai. Sabh kehnde ne nirdosh.*' (Fresh meat. Says he's innocent. Don't they all?)

The jailer sneered: '*Eh deewaaran tera sach decide karan gi, puttar.*' (These walls will decide your truth, son.)

Inside, darkness weighed down heavily.

Prisoners leered. Smugglers ran cocaine lines through the yard. Gang members carved initials into benches. Inmates whispered unspeakable things through broken smiles. Each night, Davinder hid beneath his bedding, muffling sobs—the proud kabaddi boy was reduced to tears.

Prison corrupts the weak. It destroyed his innocence, but it also birthed something more dangerous in him. Davinder had seen jails in movies: fights over food, toilets, beds; bullies trying to turn weaker boys into slaves.

One evening in the mess hall, Dhruv, the barrack's reigning bully, targeted him. He often teased Davinder, but Davinder always kept his distance. During dinner one night, Dhruv shoved Davinder's tray aside: *'Gora munda, kutteyi jhoothan wang khaa!'* (Fair boy, eat scraps like a dog!) Laughter echoed in the hall.

Davinder stood trembling. Rage surged through him. He grabbed the iron *tawa* used for roasting rotis, and in a swift move, smashed it into Dhruv's face. Blood gushed from Dhruv's nose. Panic erupted; Dhruv's gang surrounded Davinder, but none dared come near.

Davinder roared, 'Who is next?'

Then, just like in a movie, a voice from behind the crowd declared, 'Don't touch him.' It was Nishan Singh, another jail lord, from Raunkewala village. He stretched out a hand, 'I knew you'd hit this pig someday.'

The hall exploded.

Sultan Bambiha was born.

The beating of Dhruv laid the first stone for a rivalry, one that would later involve Dhruv's friend and Punjab Youth Congress leader Ravi Khwajke, and ultimately Lawrence Bishnoi. There was no turning back.

The broken boy became a man with aura and authority. Prisoners sought his approval. Two petty thieves from his village and fiercely loyal, followed him around. An old smuggler was drawn in by Davinder's defiance. Even a lifer, battered by Nishan's thugs, pledged himself to Davinder.

Unlike other jail gangs, Davinder laid down the rules. At night, huddled near a lantern, he declared: 'No drugs. No forcing boys. No cheap games. Sultan Bambiha Group stands for respect.'

His code circulated faster than fear, bred loyalty, and amid the brutality, offered something resembling justice. Soon, the prison yard echoed with his name.

When a smuggler molested a weak inmate, Davinder seized

him by the collar, threw him down, and roared: *'Jo kamzor nu chhedega... Sultan Bambiha Group usda khoon pasina ik kar dega!'* (You harm the weak, and the Sultan Bambiha Group will thrash you to pulp!)

Within days, the sobbing boy was ruling the barracks. Faridkot Jail belonged to the Sultan Bambiha Group.

Davinder did not waste his years behind rusted gates and iron bars. He studied crime the way a scholar pores over the scriptures, learning every rule, every weakness, every opportunity. What others endured as misery, he transformed into training for the future.

He carried into jail barracks the instincts of a kabaddi player. On the mud fields of Punjab, he had learned that no one man wins alone, but what makes that happen is the strength of raiders and defenders moving as one. In jail, he built his gang the same way. Some men he shaped into raiders, reckless enough to strike first, to create chaos. Others he moulded into defenders, loyal shields who protected him and crushed anyone daring to cross the line.

He carried two things with him: anger at the police and, after being betrayed by a friend, a fierce worship of loyalty. 'Anyone who offered a little empathy, any kind of help—even a piece of soap or a drop of shampoo, or a spoonful of desi ghee—was his friend for life. Davinder was eternally grateful to them. Once outside, he would kill anyone for these friends,' said his mother.

Yet one fire burnt more fiercely in him than others—his rage at the police. To anyone who would listen, he repeated the same line: 'I never pulled the trigger. I did not murder that boy.' But the system branded him a killer. That anger festered until it no longer mattered whether he had or hadn't killed Harpreet. Years later, a gang member speaking on condition of anonymity told this writer bluntly: 'By then, innocence meant nothing to him. It was long behind him.'

His mother sold her jewellery and a few acres of land to pay lawyers' fees and grease the palms of cops. 'We gave money to anyone, cop or politician, who promised to free Davinder. None kept their promise.'

Then one day, Davinder told his mother during a jail visit, 'Mother. No more money to cops. No more court cases. And don't visit me in jail. I can't stand it. I won't be here for long.'

(Years later, while still a fugitive, Davinder broke down during a media interview with journalist Yadwinder Kurfew. When asked if he missed the warmth and security of his mother's love, the feared gangster could not hold back his tears. 'Here was a man dreaded by so many, yet crying. That was when I realized just how human he truly was,' Yadwinder recalled later. The interview, however, never reached the public. Members of the Sultan Bambiha Group quickly intervened, halting the session and erasing all traces of the recording.)

The escape came on 4 September 2013.

Months earlier, the authorities had transferred Davinder and Nishan Singh along with most inmates from the district to a newly built, high-walled prison outside Faridkot. Officials thought the move would tighten control over the inmates. Instead, it set the stage for a jailbreak that would make headlines.

That evening, after a routine court appearance, Davinder and Nishan Singh were brought back with other undertrials in a dark-blue prison bus. Four policemen escorted them, their grip on their rifles lax, their alertness dulled by routine. The road leading to the gate was cut off from the main highway—so there was no place for the undertrials to run, nowhere to vanish. So convinced were the policemen that vigilance turned into complacency.

But Davinder Bambiha had gone over the escape a hundred times, rehearsing every second of it in his head.

As the line of prisoners got down from the bus and shuffled towards the gate, Bambiha deliberately stepped out of rank, his eyes locked on a car parked in the distance, its engine idling. Inside four young men waited; Dosanjh and Gurpal who were among them had recently been released on bail. They knew the jail routine like the back of their hands: the precise minutes it took for the guards to herd the prisoners inside, the dip in the vigil, the gap between caution and action.

Suddenly, the car doors burst open. The men inside leapt out, guns drawn, firing into the evening air. Sharp crackling sounds shattered the silence, scattering crows from the nearby trees. Panic seized the guards. The prisoners ducked. In the chaos, Davinder shoved past the line, with Nishan Singh close beside him.

For a heartbeat, the guards tried to block them. Then came the push—two undertrials breaking into a run, dust rising under their feet, the clamour of gunfire and orders ringing out. They charged across the open ground as if their lives still belonged to the kabaddi field.

Before the guards could regroup, Davinder and Nishan dived inside the car. The tyres screeched. The vehicle bolted forwards, swallowing the fugitives whole. Behind them, two constables lay wounded by flying bullets, clutching their legs.

By the time the dust settled and echoes of the gunfire faded, Davinder Bambiha was gone. The jail staff stood helpless within the prison walls.

Outside jail, Davinder started a relatively new trend. Not content with just carjacking or weapon-snatching, he embarked on an extortion spree, threatening not just rival gangsters on Facebook but also top police officials.

Also, it was his turn to oblige his friends. Among the first was Gurbax Sewewala. Davinder seemed to have developed a clear philosophy of life in jail: all who helped him were buddies; friends of his buddies were his friends; enemies of his buddies were his enemies. His enmity existed only because of his friends' enmity

Davinder had heard tales of the power wielded by big gangsters outside—Rocky Fazilka, Shera Khuban, Jaipal Bhullar, Lawrence Bishnoi, Vicky Gounder, among others. Many of these figures would play a big role in the making of Davinder Bambiha, the gangster. Most became rivals due to prior enmities with his friends. Some, like Vicky Gounder, had good relations with him because of mutual connections. At heart, Davinder remained a youth without personal enmity. All his killing, he justified at the altar of friendship, often declaring this in his social media posts.

His group grew quickly. New inmates, frightened and vulnerable, flocked to his fold because he offered what jail denied—protection. Names that later made it to police dossiers first appeared in his group—Gurpal Singh, Tara Singh Dosanjh, Kala Hawas, Gugni Grewal 'Meharbaan', Ranjit Sewewala, Gurbax Sewewala, and Sharni Sewewala.

In later years, he would meet hundreds more, especially Karamveer Deol, Simma Behbal Kalan, and Sukhpreet Budda—men who played key roles in making him a formidable force and eventually leading him to his nemesis. The stories of Kala Hawas, Simma Behbal Kalan, Ranjit Sewewala, and to some extent Gugni Grewal would become prominent subplots in the story of Sultan Bambiha.

◆

Davinder's first crime after escaping jail was revenge for the murder of Ranjit Sewewala.

On 9 April 2013, Ranjit Sewewala was murdered by Chamkaur Singh of Sewewala village. The reason was Chamkaur's ongoing family feud with Sharni from the same village. Sharni had sought Ranjit's help, alleging continuous harassment by Chamkaur and his uncles. Being on good terms with them, Ranjit initially avoided the conflict. However, after Sharni was beaten by the rivals, Ranjit confronted them, leading to a major clash. Village elders and the police brokered a compromise while the injured from both sides were hospitalized together. But as tensions eased, Chamkaur appeared out of nowhere and gunned down Ranjit Sewewala, lying in the hospital bed.

This brought Ranjit's brother Gurbax into the scene. A kabaddi player, Gurbax had been kept away from Ranjit's activities and had his documents ready to study abroad. The murder changed everything. Meanwhile, Chamkaur's family named Gurbax in the clash, leading to his arrest and conviction. It was while serving time in jail that Gurbax met Davinder.

Gurbax and Sharni vowed to avenge Ranjit's murder within a year. Gurbax was out on bail when Davinder escaped, and along with Simma, they began building their network—collecting money through extortion, hijacking vehicles at gunpoint, and arranging for weapons. Davinder also took control of liquor smuggling in Faridkot and in the adjoining areas.

They amassed the required weapons and funds, but, just a day before they planned the strike against Chamkaur and his relatives, police seized all their resources—guns, a car, and liquor—at a checkpoint.

Davinder was undeterred. He reminded Gurbax that Ranjit had hidden a pistol somewhere. Gurbax found it in a field—rusted and forgotten. But with Davinder's ITI welding skills, the pistol was cleaned, repaired, and made perfect for use.

Davinder drove towards the village and parked at a petrol pump overlooking the target's house and fields from the highway. Soon, he spotted Maninder Singh, 25 (Chamkaur's nephew), and Sukhpal Singh, 45 (Chamkaur's brother), riding towards the highway on a motorcycle. Both were armed.

Davinder walked towards the spot where the village mud road met the highway. The motorcycle slowed down to negotiate the turn. He called out Maninder's name. Maninder turned around.

Davinder raised his gun. Both Maninder and Sukhpal drew their weapons. The distance was more than 50 metres—enough for Davinder. He fired his pistol, hitting one in the head, earning himself the moniker of 'sharpshooter'.

Maninder reportedly died on the spot. Sukhpal was declared 'brought dead' at a private hospital in Bathinda.

Davinder then headed for Rajasthan, travelling by buses, motorcycles, cars, and a Toyota Fortuner. This was the first time he had actually killed someone. From this moment, his notoriety spread.

◆

Davinder's next target was Ravi Khwajke, who had killed his friend Kala Hawas in hospital. Kala's story opens another chapter in the rise of Punjab's gangsters from student politics and turf wars.

Kala, a resident of Hawas village in Ludhiana, had transformed from a student leader to a criminal in 2009, at a time when Davinder Bambiha was still a simple student. Ravi of Khwajke village in Ludhiana was another student leader. Ravi was close to Congress leaders, while Kala had associations with Akali leaders. Colleges in Ludhiana are affiliated with Panjab University, Chandigarh. Student politics and elections at Panjab University affected affiliated colleges too, though no student union elections were conducted in these colleges in Punjab. This was because in 1984, at the height of terrorism in Punjab, the government had banned these elections since student groups had become rallying points for terrorists, and hostels were often used as hiding grounds for wanted terrorists, and as safe houses for hiding weapons. The years of terrorism saw regular raids in college hostels.

Still, various students' associations of Panjab University had their units in affiliated colleges across Punjab. These students' groups participated in election campaigns on the university campus, providing numbers at rallies. These college units also functioned as pressure groups in elections and proved useful in brawls or in intimidating opponents. They often had the support of politicians from their respective cities as well.

In 2009, Ravi Khwajke had put up posters promoting student leaders in Panjab University elections in various colleges in Ludhiana, including Gujranwala Guru Nanak College (GGN) and Government SD College. Kala Hawas tore off these posters and pasted his own. Both became rivals, and in two years, a number of brawls took place between their groups.

However, as Ravi grew closer to senior Congress leaders—some of whom later became top politicians and ministers in the state and central governments—he started building bridges with his rivals, including Kala. As a mark of new friendship, Ravi presented a 9mm pistol to Kala. However, a few days later, police raided Kala's hideout and nabbed him with the same unlicensed pistol. Members of Kala's gang suspected Ravi of a conspiracy to get Kala arrested.

Kala is said to have given Ravi the benefit of the doubt and did not confront him. A few months later, when Kala was released on bail from Ludhiana Jail in a case, Ravi was there with his supporters to take him back home in a procession. As mentioned earlier, it had been a tradition in Punjab since the days of the first gangster Dimpy Chandbhan to flaunt one's power and following by lining up a cavalcade of vehicles to celebrate jail releases.

Ravi was, however, surprised to see that many other groups had already gathered to welcome Kala. Still, Kala sat in Ravi's Pajero—a rage in those days. Gangsters close to both sides, as well as police groups, claimed Ravi became jealous of Kala's following. Kala was the main strongman in the area, capable of challenging Ravi's growth. By now, Ravi had already become the sarpanch of his village. Meanwhile, Kala reportedly met some top Akali leaders—a cause for concern among Congress leaders and Ravi.

Another reason for the growing rift between Ravi and Kala was the latter's closeness to Davinder Bambiha. Meanwhile, Ravi maintained ties with other top gangsters like Jaipal Bhullar and Vicky Gounder.

On 11 June 2015, Davinder was arrested in Ludhiana after an encounter. Just past dawn that day, Faridkot Police had closed in on him.Wanted in two brutal murder cases and known for his daring escape from custody in 2013, Davinder had been under surveillance via mobile tracking for a while. The police team led by DSP Sukhdev Singh Brar, had been tailing Davinder and his accomplice Gursharan Singh from Faridkot. The chase reached a flashpoint near Bhaiwala Chowk, Ludhiana, where the police intercepted their vehicle. Gursharan bolted from the car, vanishing into the streets, while Davinder, cornered and desperate, opened fire. Nearly 25 rounds were fired before Davinder was hit in the arm.

Wounded but not subdued, Davinder fled to a nearby house, attempting to vanish once more into the shadows. But the police, relentless and prepared, tracked him down and made the arrest. They found a pistol and 21 bullets on him—proof that he was ready for a prolonged stand-off. The capture was a major breakthrough, especially considering his dramatic escape two years ago. Since then, the Faridkot Police had scoured Hazoor Sahib, Nanded, and Gujarat, chasing leads in a manhunt spanning several states.

Davinder spent a few weeks in Ludhiana Jail before being shifted to Faridkot Jail, where a number of court cases were pending against him.

While in jail, Davinder got the news that on September 6, four persons on two motorcycles had shot down Kala Hawas, who was travelling in a car on Rahon Road.

That very day, Davinder vowed vengeance.

◆

In Ludhiana Jail, Davinder Bambiha met Karamveer Deol, another student leader closely linked to Lawrence Bishnoi. It is believed that Karamveer, who later moved to the US on a fake passport, helped Davinder procure weapons, and promised assistance in fleeing abroad. Police officials later stated that Karamveer became an expert in preparing fake passports. He successfully migrated and also helped Anmol

Bishnoi, Lawrence Bishnoi's brother, escape to the US on forged documents. Anmol was even spotted attending a wedding reception for Karamveer in California—an event made special by Punjabi singer Karan Aujla's performance.

At the time, Davinder had forged valuable connections and harboured no personal enmity against Lawrence, nor was Davinder inclined to merge his gang with Lawrence's. However, all this would change with matters involving Ravi Khwajke. But before that, Davinder would commit another murder.

Shortly after Davinder was moved to Faridkot Jail due to the numerous court trials pending in the district court there, he met new allies, as often happens with every jail transfer, widened his network, and inevitably made new rivals. It was in Faridkot Jail that he met Simma Behbal Kalan, a lovelorn youth claiming harassment by relatives of his fiancée.

In the quiet villages of Punjab, Harsimrandeep Singh—known as Simma from Behbal Kalan—found his life entangled in love, betrayal, and vengeance. It began in 2008 when his maternal uncle, Swarn Singh, and the matchmaker Beant Singh arranged his engagement to Parminder Kaur, daughter of Rachhpal Singh from Moga. The alliance seemed promising. Harsimrandeep and Parminder remained in touch over phone calls and occasionally met in Ludhiana, where she studied and he was preparing for IELTS (International English Language Testing System). But fate had other plans. Parminder's family, enticed by opportunities abroad, relocated to Canada with the help of Harsimrandeep's maternal grandparents who were already Canadian residents. Once settled there, Parminder's family began dodging questions on the engagement and eventually denied it outright. Beant Singh, the maternal uncle who brokered the match, turned cold and instructed Harsimrandeep's father to cease all contact. The rejection stung deeply but what followed was worse.

One fateful day in 2012, as Harsimrandeep rode to Maheshwari for dog races, Beant spotted him and unleashed his men. They ambushed Harsimrandeep between Desh Bhagat College and LLR College, dragging him off his motorcycle and beating him mercilessly. They seized his phone and deleted all the cherished photos of him and Parminder.

For months, Harsimrandeep waited in vain, farming his fields in 2013 and pleading his case through intermediaries, but Beant and Parminder's grandfather, Kartar Singh, rebuffed every appeal, dashing any hope of reconciliation.

By 2014, desperation led Harsimrandeep down dark alleys. A dispute involving his friend Pargat Singh drew him into an armed confrontation, resulting in his arrest under the Arms Act (1959) after the police stopped their car near Bajakhana. Jailed in Faridkot for seven days, he crossed paths with Gursharanjeet Singh (Sharni Sewewala) and his father Roop Singh, who shared a barrack with notorious gangster Davinder Bambiha. Through Roop, Harsimrandeep got a glimpse of the underworld—a meeting that would soon set him on the path to retribution. After being released on bail, and to allay his family's fears, he isolated himself at home in his native village for six months.

The turning point came in January 2015 when Davinder escaped from custody. Two months later, his associate Bunty appeared at Harsimrandeep's door, luring him to a waiting Hyndai Verna in which sat Davinder. They had gone to demand money from Latu, but the plan had failed. Weeks later, on a dusty road between Bargari and Kotkapura, Davinder's group flagged Harsimrandeep down, seeking shelter. He led them to his maternal grandparents' house that was vacant in Niwan. Here Bunty recounted Harsimrandeep's tale of heartbreak. Davinder's eyes narrowed as Harsimrandeep named Beant as the tormentor. 'We'll take care of him,' Davinder promised, his words laced with lethal intent.

The alliance grew stronger. They hid in villages like Gill Kalan and Gurusar, evading the authorities. In May 2015, Bunty summoned Harsimrandeep to a common friend's place, arming him with a .22 bore revolver while Davinder carried a .32. Twice they stalked Beant in Vadda Ghar, but he eluded them. A detour to a village brawl in Bargadi saw them firing shots to disperse their foes, forging their bond through chaos.

Finally, at dawn, on a crisp May morning, they struck. After parking near a drain outside Vadda Ghar, they confirmed Beant's location through an associate. As Beant drove home, Harsimrandeep overtook him in the Hyundai Verna, blocking his path. Davinder leapt out, unleashing four fatal shots from his .32 revolver. Beant slumped dead, his spilt blood ending Harsimrandeep's long-simmering agony.

In the aftermath, Davinder and Harsimrandeep fled to Sirsa, holing up at a Congress MLA's house.

◆

Harsimrandeep or Simma Behbal Kalan would become one of Punjab's most wanted gangsters-turned-terrorists. His association with Davinder and his first murder—of Beant Singh—marked the beginning of his rise in crime. He would lead the Sultan Bambiha Group for some time, remaining closely allied with Davinder in his lifetime. Initially, he led the Sewewala gang (named after Ranjit of Sewewala village), and all these gangs worked together.

Simma is presently a Category-A gangster and a wanted fugitive. Police records state he fled abroad on fake documents. He made headlines for brutally beating up some people accused of sacrilege in Punjab, earning the support of Sikh hardliner groups.

With over 26 criminal cases registered against him, including murder, extortion, and drug trafficking, Simma has built a reputation for being ruthless. His criminal career gained notoriety after the 2017 murder of a rice miller in Jaito. Arrested in Dehradun in 2018 during a joint operation by Punjab and Uttarakhand police, he repeatedly secured bail and returned to Behbal Kalan, where his presence continues to intimidate locals.

In 2024, Simma made headlines again when he allegedly intimidated villagers to ensure his father's unopposed election as sarpanch. Such was the fear that he had instilled in them that no one dared to file nomination papers for the panchayat elections. Though his father did not officially contest, the absence of other candidates underscored Simma's grip over the village. His associates were caught with illegal weapons, and the police were able to link him to several planned dacoities and gang activities, including connections to the Sultan Bambiha Group.

Simma's influence extends beyond street crime. In May 2023, the National Investigation Agency seized ₹39 lakh from his residence, indicating widespread financial networks.

◆

Davinder tried twice before to kill Ravi—once at a wedding attended by senior Congress leaders, where heavy security forced him to abandon the plan, and again at a kabaddi match where Ravi was the chief guest, but the presence of private gunmen stopped Davinder from carrying out the attack.

On 20 February 2016, Davinder finally got his chance at Gill Garden—a resort on the Ludhiana-Malerkotla road—where Ravi was attending a wedding. As he sat on a chair outside the venue with his friend Balwinder Singh, a group of armed men emerged and opened fire. Ravi took 14 bullets, while Balwinder was injured but survived. There was panic at the crime scene. After killing Ravi, the assailants, instead of fleeing, danced at the spot in front of the stunned guests and fired roughly 50 rounds in the air in a brazen display of arrogance. The entire incident was captured on CCTV and became crucial evidence in the investigation.

Davinder called Gugni Grewal in jail, saying, 'Announce in the jail—Ravi Khwajke is dead. Bambiha has killed him.'

Among the shooters was Avtar Singh alias Tari from Dosanjh village, Moga, who was later convicted and sentenced to life imprisonment. Kamaljit Singh alias Bunty and Jaspreet Singh alias Jumpy, also involved in the shooting, were killed in separate police encounters before the trial. Sukhchain Singh, alias Gopi, who had been tailing Ravi Khwajke and identified him at the wedding, fled abroad after the murder. He was later arrested in Malaysia and is facing a separate trial.

Other alleged conspirators included Dharminder Singh alias Gugni, Kirpal Singh alias Pala, and Navpreet Singh alias Novi, all accused of helping hatch the plot from inside jail, but they were acquitted for lack of evidence.

Additional names surfaced during investigations—Navpreet Singh Cheema alias Noni, Karamveer Singh, Jassi (brother of slain gangster Kala Hawas), and Mandip Singh alias Mandeep Bawa.

'This is just a trailer. More is coming,' declared Davinder on a Facebook post after the murder. With this killing, he had become Punjab's top gangster. Punjab Police had at that time not formed any specialized police unit to tackle gangsters. The Counter-Intelligence Wing, which monitored terrorism and cross-border smuggling, handled gangsters as well.

Until then, it was the district police's responsibility to track gangsters active in their areas. Davinder used to hide out in Rampura Phul town, in Bathinda District, where SSP Swapan Sharma headed the force.

In the early hours of 9 September 2016, the fields near Gill Kalan village, close to Rampura Phul in Bathinda, became the stage for a dramatic showdown. Punjab Police, acting on a tip-off, surrounded a farmhouse where Davinder Singh alias Bambiha—Punjab's most wanted gangster—was hiding with his aide Tara Dosanjh. Davinder, then just 25, had become infamous for a string of murders, including the high-profile killing of sarpanch Ravi Khwajke, and had become a social media sensation by openly taunting the police.

The operation was led by SSP Swapan Sharma, a 2009-batch IPS officer of Punjab cadre. Born in Kangra, Himachal Pradesh, Sharma had built a reputation as an 'encounter specialist', known for being calm under fire and relentless in his pursuit of organized crime.

In the weeks leading up to the encounter, Punjab Police intensified their hunt for Davinder, not only for his involvement in high-profile murders but due to a brazen act that embarrassed the police—Davinder had recently hijacked a police officer's vehicle. The officer—alone and in plain clothes—tried reasoning with Davinder, revealing his identity as a cop. Unfazed, Davinder reportedly replied, 'I am Sultan Bambiha, the sharpshooter,' before speeding away in the stolen vehicle. The incident threw a direct challenge to the police force's authority, underscoring the urgency to nab Davinder.

•

SSP Sharma's journey to the IPS was remarkable. He cracked the Civil Services Exam, and chose Punjab cadre, quickly rising through the ranks due to his hands-on approach and commitment to public safety. Over his career, he was involved in nearly 50 encounters, often facing threats from gangsters who openly challenged him on social media, earning him the title 'Encounter Specialist' of Punjab Police.

On 9 September 2016, acting on a tip-off, Sharma and his teams surrounded the farmhouse near Gill Kalan. Two CIA teams led by Sharma cordoned off the area at 4 a.m. As the police closed in, Davinder and his aide tried to escape, abandoning their car and fleeing into the paddy fields. A fierce four-hour gunfight followed, with over 70 rounds exchanged. Davinder, armed and desperate, fired at the police, who returned fire with precision.

Davinder took three bullets in the chest and collapsed in the fields. He was declared brought dead at Bathinda Civil Hospital. His associate Tara Dosanjh was wounded in the encounter and arrested.

Davinder's mother learnt of the news on TV. Her only son was no more. She had woven dreams of his freedom and happiness. Was he free in death? She would later question many who came to mourn.

Weeks later, she had her son's name inscribed atop their two-storeyed house.

The first thing one notices on entering the courtyard is the name painted in blue: not Davinder Singh Sidhu, as she had named him, but Davinder Bambiha, the name the world gave her son.

10

Lawrence Bishnoi

SOMETIME IN AUGUST 2011, JARNAIL Singh, weathered with age and endless rounds of courts and police stations, stood under a tree in the premises of a Panchkula (Haryana) court. His son, Shera Khuban, his lifeline, had become a shadow. A gangster, Shera's name echoed as the 'Badshah' of the underworld after the infamous Panchkula bank robbery case.

He, along with notorious highway robber Jaipal Bhullar, their common buddy Chandu, and Tinu Rana (son of a Chandigarh Police Sub-Inspector) stormed into the Sector 15 State Bank of Patiala in Panchkula. They did not even bother to mask their faces—a rare audacity for a bank heist. The four gangsters then decamped with ₹9.57 lakh.

Shera was scheduled to reach the court for a hearing in the Panchkula bank robbery case. He was the prime accused. Jarnail Singh would crane his neck now and then to look for the police van—its blue colour, and windows covered with an iron mesh, distinct even from a distance.

God knows he had tried to steer Shera away from the path of crime. But fate, like a relentless river, swept them both downstream.

'What could I have done differently?' Singh questioned himself, tracing the lines on his wrinkled palms.

'Betrayal of trust,' a voice came from some deep crevice

in his heart. The father was sad. His son had betrayed his trust—that he would not go astray, that he would bring fame not infamy to the family.

In between those moments of despair, Singh had clung on to one hope—that society would embrace his son, not condemn him.

Sab theek ho jayega (Everything will be alright), Singh had reassured himself, even as Shera's footsteps echoed down the wrong corridors.

Singh moved towards his son; the police also allowed them to chat. The men in khaki understand that a few minutes with the family will help the 'beast' they had brought in handcuffs, to be at relative peace for several days in the lock-up or, more urgently, on the way back to the jail. So, sometimes, out of humanity, they allow a brief chat with a family member. Other times, a few pieces of coloured paper bearing Mahatma Gandhi's face do the persuading.

What wouldn't have Singh given at that moment to hug his son for as long as he wanted. 'Not much time. Stay at a distance,' the police said as Singh wondered what would emerge first—words from his throat or tears from his eyes.

'Are you okay?' he asked his son.

Shera nodded but looked here and there as if he wanted to see someone else.

Somehow Singh managed to assure his son in Punjabi, '*Sab theek ho jayega, puttar.*' (All will be well, son.)

Shera's eyes brightened up as he waved at something behind his father—a group of youths, who were awestruck at the sight of Shera, their hero. As the police looked the other way, Shera's followers offered him gifts—dry fruits, expensive shirts, sports shoes—innumerable symbols of their unwavering allegiance to him.

In that moment, Singh understood how Shera could have been saved.

'Intervention,' he murmured. Perhaps that was the missing piece—a mentor, a guiding hand, or simply society at large. Someone to untangle the knots in Shera's soul. But the system failed them both.

Among the youths crowding his son, one boy stood apart. Fair-skinned, with a neat haircut, expensive clothes and sports shoes, and muscular arms; though of medium height, he had a towering presence. There was a special spark in his eyes—a hunger for purpose, a longing to belong. He sat close to Shera, slowly cracking open pistachio shells and feeding him with his hands.

Who is he? Singh wondered, keeping an eye on him even when the police whisked Shera away to the courtroom. As the group dispersed, the handsome youth waited.

'Who are you, son?' Singh had to know him.

'Uncle Ji, I am from your area only. My name is Lawrence,' he said, smiling.

The smile touched something deep within Singh. *Wait,* he told himself, *I am searching for an intervention for my son, whereas I am the intervention. I can stop these youths who are drawn to Shera by the tales of his 'bravado', or who have been forced by circumstances into becoming rebels.* Singh was determined to save Lawrence. But first he had to get to know him.

'What are you doing here? Why are you feeding my son? Who are you?' So many questions tumbled out of his mouth.

'Uncle Ji, I am from your region—Dutaranwali village,' the youth said, touching the elder's feet as a mark of respect. He still sported that inimitable smile that Singh would see later in several videos of the gangster.

'I am like a brother to Shera bhaaji. He is a legend, a superhero,' Lawrence insisted. 'Our villages are but a whisper apart. Dutaranwali and Khuban—they share the same soil, the same blood.'

'I am studying in Chandigarh,' Lawrence continued.

Singh heaved a sigh of relief. Would he follow the path of Law?

'We have about 110 acres of land. We are Bishnois,' said Lawrence. Before Singh could say anything more to him, they heard a commotion near the court room. Shera had come out of the trial court. He gesticulated to his father, indicating that he hadn't been granted bail. The police whisked him away towards the waiting van. Singh somehow managed to hand over to Shera some money, a 2 kg tin of desi ghee and another tin of *panjeeri* (a sweet dish) cooked by Shera's mother. 'Take care, son. And look after your health. I will talk to the lawyers,' Singh shouted after him.

By the time Singh looked back, the fair-skinned youth too had left.

Jarnail Singh kept thinking about Lawrence all day. There was a certain fire in his eyes, an ambition which he had seen in his own son's eyes too. Next morning, he set out for Dutaranwali village. The name of the village means 'place of two stars' (do means 'two' and tara means 'star'). In everyday usage, Dutaranwali became Dutranwali. Sadly, two brothers from the village would make headlines for all the wrong reasons: Lawrence and young brother Anmol, both have Red Corner Interpol notices against them.

Singh had to warn the Bishnois. On the way, he called up a friend from the same village and learnt all he could about them. Lawrence's parents were rich, as he already knew from the 110 acres of land they had. They were a large and connected family. An uncle was even a serving judge in Ambala Sessions Court.

The Bishnoi household met Singh but not with much warmth. As he shared his meeting with Lawrence the day before, and revealed that the purpose of the visit was to warn them, Lawrence's mother broke into sobs. The father who had not uttered a word seemed to shrink further into his cocoon.

Singh's words hung heavy in the air.

'You still have time,' he told them. 'Unlike me, you can pull him back from the abyss. But hope is a fragile thing—it slips through our fingers like sand.'

Lawrence's mother clutched her prayer beads, her entreaties to the Almighty a desperate plea. Lawrence's father stared blankly into the distance. After hearing what Singh had to say, they bid him a silent farewell.

◆

Lawrence, undoubtedly the most talked-about gangster in Punjab in present times with nearly 80 cases against him, has spoken through a number of posts on social media, besides audio messages and even a TV interview from police custody. Sometimes, he has done a U-turn in the court of law, denying all those claims. Following his media interview, the government banned all media interaction with him. His diary, whose authenticity has been confirmed by Lawrence's uncle Ramesh Bishnoi besides Punjab Police officials, provides a glimpse into the gangster's mind:[8]

---

[8]The author is in possession of the diary pages referred to in this chapter.

My parents pampered me from day one. They fulfilled all my wishes, bought me anything I wanted. It could be clothes or a motorcycle, or even a car or a school, a college [where] I wanted to study. Perhaps, that is why they gave in to my persistent demands to join a school and later a college in Chandigarh [about 350 km from his village, Dutaranwali]. And that is where began the new chapter of my life. I look back and would say I wasn't ready for the big city, coming from a village; its flashy high-flying [life]style. I had not seen my schoolmates back home going to pubs and discos and hookah bars. I was a simple guy who wore what my mother chose for me and was happy with the monthly pocket money I received. My life pace was slow, like a bicycle till the big city happened. My parents wanted me out of the village for a better education. And at the tender age of ten, I was sent to boarding to get the best education and make them proud, at my aunt's house (Bua ji—father's sister). Instead, and contrary to their dreams, I became a criminal.

I was merely 17, when I saw the inside of a jail for the first time in my life. I blame the high-speed life in Chandigarh, like a fast-flying aeroplane, as I, peddling my bicycle, tried to match it. In the city, I made many friends and foes, and I would say I was not an equal to them, even though my father is the biggest landlord in our village. In order to match up to those friends and enemies, I have become such a man that my mother has to pass through the police of three states to meet me. Security agencies eavesdrop on our phone conversations. This is so opposite to the love-filled days of my school hostel life. My mother would come to take me home for holidays and drop me back at her will. And now I am called one of the most dangerous criminals and a threat to public peace. Time and situation never remain the same for a man. Now, she has to pass through several security checks for a few minutes of conversation with me. And with whom should I share the aches of my heart. I cannot meet her when I long for it. I don't have that freedom.

Only my god knows if I am a powerful Bahubali or a helpless man.

Sometimes I wonder what people really say about me, or [if they] fear me as [the] media and [the] police say. When I hear such kind of talks about me, I also succumb to the illusion that I am a big shot or something. I even feel proud of myself. But God doesn't let me stay in that zone for long. He shows me the truth and that is why I spend more time in his worship than anything else.

And [the] rest of the time, I spend doing my Karm—the actions I am supposed to do, which people term criminal acts. I do not believe I am bigger than anyone. My ideals are martyrs. I am just a simple man who doesn't take any injustice, or bow my head before anyone and who will always respond to [the] challenge for a battle. My God will decide the matter of life and death, victory or defeat. We should leave such talks. I am succumbing to feelings and emotions. I do not know about these. I have no experience. I wanted to talk about my brother Bhanu.

Bhanu is the nickname of Anmol Bishnoi, Lawrence's brother who is six years younger than him. He is an accused in at least 18 cases of murder, extortion, and forgery. He fled India in April and was living illegally in the United States, wearing an anklet monitor and under periodic scrutiny by local police

In November 2025, Anmol was located in the US during a coordinated crackdown on fugitives and undocumented migrants. He was wanted in India for his alleged role in several high-profile crimes, including the firing outside actor Salman Khan's residence and multiple extortion conspiracies. US authorities detained him, verified his identity and cleared him for deportation.

On 18 November 2025, Anmol Bishnoi was deported to India along with nearly 200 other Indian nationals. He was taken into custody by the NIA as soon as he landed at Delhi's Indira Gandhi International Airport. His return marked a significant breakthrough in India's efforts to dismantle the Bishnoi gang's transnational operations, as he had allegedly been coordinating criminal activities from abroad. He has since been in NIA custody, with investigations focusing on threats to celebrities, extortion rackets, and political killings.

Before his arrest, another major development had already put him on national radar. On 27 April 2024, Mumbai Police issued a lookout circular (LOC) against him following the shooting incident outside Salman Khan's Galaxy Apartments residence in Bandra, Mumbai, in April 2024. Mumbai Police classified the firing as warning shots. Anmol plublicly claimed responsibility for the attack, saying it was the first and last warning from him to the actor.

The act was part of a longer chain of hostility. Lawrence had earlier sent shooters on at least two occasions to kill Salman Khan as retaliation for the 1998 blackbuck poaching case, in which the actor was accused of killing the animals considered sacred by the Bishnoi community.

The first major attempt took place on 14 April 2024, when two armed men fired multiple rounds outside Galaxy Apartments. No one was injured, but investigators viewed it as a deliberate escalation from previous written and verbal threats.

This followed a series of ominous developments, including threatening letters and trespassing attempts at Khan's Panvel farmhouse. The second attempt was more indirect but equally menacing. On 10 July, 7 August, and 16 October 2025, Kapil Sharma's café—Kap's Café—in Surrey, Canada, was attacked twice by gunmen allegedly linked to the Bishnoi gang. The reason? Anyone collaborating with Salman Khan—including Kapil Sharma, who had invited Khan to launch his show on Netflix—would face consequences. In the second attack, around 25 rounds were fired, but no injuries were reported.

Leaked audio recordings later revealed that Bishnoi's associate, Harry Boxer, had issued warnings to Bollywood personalities against working with Salman Khan. These attacks were not just personal vendettas but strategic moves to isolate Khan professionally and instill fear within the entertainment industry.

Elsewhere in his diary, Lawrence has written:

> My younger brother Bhanu would prefer spending time with me than with friends of his age. He would follow me in wedding parties or elsewhere. When I asked him why he didn't play with his classmates or other kids, he would just say he liked being with me. He has been my shadow since I remember. It is truly said that a devoted brother who becomes your friend is a blessing. It was for me, but inadvertently he followed me on the path of crime as well. Despite my all efforts that he should live a normal life, he too became a partner in crime. And followed me into this world of no return.

There has never been a moment in my life when my heartbeat had not increased at the mention of his name. Or if I had not wept for him. Like other siblings, we too used to have fights and I abused him too but never ever has it happened that I will not remember him. Perhaps only when I die or may be not. He has never ever talked back to me. He would always smile at my rebukes. He would say he was always with me and would remain so, no matter whatever I did, he would be proud to be my younger brother.

But knowingly or unknowingly, like hundreds of other youths, Bhanu too followed me into the world of crime. He got attracted to this world because of me and when I realized [that], it was too late for me. I could do nothing to save him or the hundreds of other youths who became part of these gang battles. Many like my old friend Sampat even put their life on the line for me. They left their homes and family for me. Sometimes I wonder how many lives would be destroyed because of me but I can't stop now as I have to continue following my path.

My friends Sampat, Naresh and Sachin Thapan have done so much for me that I can give my life for them and I can take anyone's life for them. For me, nothing is bigger than friendship.

I had so much to write—a poem, a couplet, but maybe some other time, as now, I have to send this diary out of jail. I will write again if I remain alive.

Ram Ram
Jai Hanuman.

◆

Lawrence Bishnoi has several pages dedicated to him on

Facebook. He has a huge following, especially in the Abohar-Fazilka-Ganganagar belt of Punjab and Rajasthan. At 5'6", with a strong muscular built, Lawrence has an oval face, sports a neatly kept beard and a thick mop of black hair that accentuates his fair skin and the angular jawline. Under other circumstances, he could have tried a career in modelling.

But behind that veneer of pleasantness is a cold-blooded killer.

Sidhu Moosewala: A Voice Silenced (29 May 2022)

In broad daylight, Punjabi singer and Congress leader Sidhu Moosewala was ambushed and shot dead in Mansa, Punjab. The attack, carried out by gang members allegedly under Lawrence's orders, was a brutal response to a perceived betrayal and a show of dominance in ongoing gang wars. Moosewala's death sent shockwaves across India, exposing the fine lines between celebrityhood, politics, and organized crime.

Hardeep Singh Nijjar: A Killing That Crossed Borders (18 June 2023)

Outside a gurdwara in Surrey, Canada, Khalistani activist Hardeep Singh Nijjar was gunned down. While the Royal Canadian Mounted Police investigated multiple leads, Lawrence's gang emerged as a suspected player. The murder started a diplomatic storm between India and Canada, with Nijjar's death becoming a flashpoint in debates over transnational extremism and gang influence. Canada officially declared Lawrence Bishnoi and his gang a terrorist entity on 29 September 2025.

Nadir Shah: The Gymfront Execution (12 September 2024)

Dubai-based entrepreneur Nadir Shah was shot dead outside his gym in Delhi's upscale Greater Kailash I neighbourhood. The hit was allegedly coordinated by Randeep Malik, a Bishnoi associate operating from the US, who lured Shah outside the gym moments before the shooting. The murder exposed glaring lapses in Delhi Police's counter-intelligence operations, and highlighted the gang's international coordination.

Baba Siddique: The Political Hit (12 October 2024)

Former Maharashtra minister Baba Siddique was assassinated in Mumbai in what appeared to be a contract killing. The Bishnoi gang claimed responsibility through social media posts by associate Shubham Lonkar. Though the motive remains speculative, investigators believe the hit was tied to an extortion bid and political rivalries, underscoring the gang's reach in elite circles.

Sukhdool Singh: The Shadow War in Canada (2024)

Another Canada-based Khalistani figure, Sukhdool Singh, was reportedly assassinated in what some believe was a gangland-style killing. Though the details remain murky, Lawrence's network was suspected of involvement, possibly driven by ideological rivalry or turf wars. The killing added to the growing list of overseas operations linked to the gang.

The Club Bombings: Terror as a Business Model (November–December 2024)

Though not targeted killings, the bombings outside Seville Bar (owned by singer Badshah), De'Orra Club in Chandigarh, and several nightclubs in Gurugram were calculated acts of terror. Orchestrated by Lawrence's network, these attacks were meant to extort money and intimidate Bollywood figures. Again, Randeep Malik was suspected of arranging the explosives and coordinating shooters from abroad. Add to that, a master plotter who rules not just the Punjab gangs but is part of a national syndicate of gangsters as well.

Bharat Ratan alias Vicky: The Cross-Border Killers (20 September 2025)

In Fazilka, Punjab, a leading clothes merchant, Bharat Ratan, was murdered by Bishnoi operatives who fled to Nepal immediately after. Their return, allegedly under instructions from foreign handlers to commit another 'sensational crime', led to their arrest on the Patiala-Ambala highway. The case revealed the gang's ability to operate across borders with impunity.

◆

While Dimpy Chandbhan and Rocky Fazilka partnered with Uttar Pradesh gangsters, Lawrence set up a syndicate of gangs that operated from the national capital—New Delhi—with a network spread across India and abroad, especially Canada, USA, Dubai and Pakistan. There is a long list of ransoms paid to Lawrence Bishnoi by industrialists, businessmen, jewellers and contractors of various projects. But officially he has just

₹80,000 in his Punjab National Bank account in Abohar, as per the police records of 2022–23. Where is all the ransom money parked? A question no security agency has been able to answer so far.

Yet, in the police dossier on him, Lawrence says his future plan is to leave the world of crime and live in peace.

That sounds unbelievable given his bloody track record, the topmost crime perhaps being the murder of singer Sidhu Moosewala, whose parents Balkaur Sidhu and Charan Kaur live with this tragedy every single moment, as they seek a death sentence for Lawrence.

◆

Lawrence Bishnoi could not have dreamt of a better house to be born into. His parents owned about 110 acres of land in Dutaranwali village in Abohar. The name of the village means 'place of two stars' (*do* means two and *tara* means star). In everyday usage, Dutaranwali became Dutranwali. Sadly, two brothers from the village have made headlines for all the wrong reasons. Lawrence and young brother Anmol, both have Red Corner Interpol notices against them.

If the ancestral property was not enough, Lawrence's father Lakhwinder Bishnoi and his mother Sunita Bishnoi nurtured big dreams for him. Due to his exceptionally fair complexion, different from the usual wheatish complexion of Punjab boys, Sunita christened him Lawrence after British officer, educationist and social reformer Henry Lawrence. She dreamt of seeing her son as a reputed officer whether in the armed forces or in civil administration. Instead, she sees him handcuffed, surrounded by either men in khaki or commandos in black uniforms. Instead of plush offices, Lawrence sits in police lock-ups and dingy jail cells, and travels in rickety police vans rather than the swanky high-end cars they could easily afford.

They never wanted him to stay in the village. So, they sent him for schooling up to Middle level (Class VIII) in MRM School, Ajmer, in Rajasthan. Lawrence had six paternal aunts—all married into respectable families in various districts of Rajasthan. They too dreamt of a great future for the eldest son of their only brother.

In Punjab or Haryana, having a male child was, and perhaps still is, considered a blessing from God and, though to a lesser degree today, is preferred over a female child. The Bathinda-Mansa-Abohar belt has a feudal and patriarchal mindset where boys are pampered. It is not uncommon to see families where parents produce one child after another till they get a male child—the one who will carry forward the family's name. It is not unusual to stumble upon many families that had two to five or even more daughters before they had a son, and stopped reproducing after that.

Bishnoi combines two Marwari words—*bis* meaning 20 and *noi* meaning 9. These 29 *niyamas* (tenets) form the origin of the Bishnoi community and govern their lifestyle. These dictate how a Bishnoi must follow personal hygiene, ensure social behaviour, dedicate themselves to worship, preserve biodiversity, and protect animals.

The community was founded by Guru Jambeshwar (Guru Jambho Ji) in the early 15th century in Rajasthan. The community members are known as the first eco-warriors. As many as 363 Bishnois sacrificed their life in 1730 protecting Khejri trees from being axed in Khejarli village in Rajasthan. The then Maharaja of Jodhpur, Abhai Singh, needed the wood to build a new palace. A Bishnoi woman, Amrita Devi, hugged a tree to protect it. Besides trees, the community also worships the blackbuck.

It is difficult to understand why Lawrence, coming from a community known for its non-violent ways, took to violence in the extreme form—threatening to kill Bollywood star Salman Khan for allegedly poaching two blackbucks.

'There have been instances of violence, including murders, whenever someone challenges our self-respect and pride. Bishnois have killed people to save the family name, just like other communities in Punjab, Rajasthan or anywhere for that matter,' says Ramesh Bishnoi, Lawrence's uncle.

After Class VIII, Lawrence's parents got him admitted in Assumption Convent School, Abohar, in order to have their teenage son close by. But Lawrence insisted on studying in a big city like Chandigarh for higher education and the parents gave in. He got admission in DAV School, Sector 15, for his higher secondary certificate, and it is here that his life changed—'A new chapter began,' as he wrote in his diary.

In Chandigarh, besides the high-flying life, the discos and clubs he came across, Lawrence was exposed to the student election politics of Panjab University, Chandigarh—the same politics from where gangsters like Dimpy Chandbhan and Rocky Fazilka emerged.

It is common for youths finding themselves lost in a big city to join a group of boys belonging to their native place. Lawrence found one such friend—or an 'elder brother', as he says—in Vicky Middukhera, who belonged to the Student Organisation of Panjab University (SOPU). Vicky's village Middukhera falls in the Abohar belt of Punjab, about 30 km from Lawrence's village Dutaranwali. Shera's village Khuban sits roughly in the middle of these two villages. Another gangster Vicky Gounder's village Sarwan Bolda too is in the same axis.

Lawrence came to the city aiming to study Law. His parents also wished he would study Law and perhaps follow in the footsteps of his uncle, the serving judge at the Sessions Court.

What they got instead was a name etched in police dossiers, whispered in courtrooms, and shouted in gang-war ultimatums, operating with at least one fake ID—Balkaran Singh Brar, son of Azad Singh.

Lawrence arrived in Chandigarh, confident and restless, rooted in the feudal mindset of rural Punjab. He joined DAV Model School, which was a good start. But in a city where identity was forged by ambition and class, Lawrence fumbled. Around him were students chasing the civil services dreams, the MBAs and other degrees with global currency. He searched for validation elsewhere—in speed, muscle, loyalty, fear. Two years in DAV School and then in DAV College—he never completed his graduation.

Lawrence met Vicky Middukhera on the playgrounds of Panjab University. Lawrence would practise the 1,500-metre race. That became a long and deep association involving attempts to dominate student politics not just in Chandigarh but in entire Punjab. That involved brawls, gunshots and included the murder of Vicky Middukhera—a crime by Lawrence's rivals, but which led to the daylight killing of Punjabi rapper Sidhu Moosewala.

Lawrence had no dearth of money. From motorcycles he graduated to a Mahindra Bolero even while he was studying in DAV School. He had everything but a circle to move in. Vicky Middukhera took him under his wing. Lawrence tended to prove his mettle by indulging in violence, providing his SUV and other resources for rallies. But it was his daredevil leadership of the youth that contributed to his rise.

In April 2010, violence followed a student election. Lawrence and his associate, Sampat Nehra (who would try to kill Salman Khan many years down the line), backed a candidate named Robin Brar for DAV College Union president. The rival camp—affiliated to PUSU—stood in their way. The Robin Brar group won the elections. But the rivalry had already turned into enmity.

Lawrence's response? Bullets. A car was set on fire. Lawrence wanted to make a mark and led the assault.

What followed was incarceration in Burail Jail, Chandigarh. But it wasn't punishment. It was orientation. There, through crackling prison wires and clanging steel doors, he met arms smuggler Ranjit Dupla and crime lord Rocky Fazilka. Lessons weren't taught; they were absorbed. He studied gang structures, interstate alliances, the price of guns, and the weight of betrayal. From behind bars, he started plotting a new underworld. Not a street gang but a syndicate. Not just Punjab but the world. If only Indian jails were able to isolate young minds like Lawrence from hardened criminals, many a bright spark could still be saved.

Punjabi actor and music director Sonu Bajwa would recall in media interviews seeing Lawrence and big names of Punjab gangsterism. He was in the jail with them.

A leader of musclemen at that time, Sonu towered over a large group of youths, including bouncers, who dealt in recovery of cars whose owners defaulted on bank loans. Sonu often provided for his young powerful group of men in the power show of student elections and rallies. He was jailed with Lawrence Bishnoi, Shera Khuban, Jaipal Bhullar and others.

And he saw their following in the jail. All had a following but not Lawrence. Not yet.

'When after a brawl we had to surrender to the police, Lawrence insisted on joining us. He was not even in college at that time. He was just a school student. But he was in the lead, burning vehicles of rival candidates. "*Bhai Ji, tuhade naal hi jaana*," (Brother, I wish to go with you) he insisted. In jail we met Shera, who spent most of the time exercising. And Jaipal, who would be found reading. He rarely spoke. And Lawrence—a devotee of Hanuman Ji—used to spend time chanting. He would amaze us by performing 108 *surya namaskar*s and sitting in meditation.'

Yet, he was distraught when no one came to greet him when he got bail in the case. 'He was the first to get bail within a month or so, whereas we got it after three months,' Sonu recalled in media interviews. It was a tradition that student leaders who got bail would be received by hundreds, even thousands, and taken back to their university in a procession of cars. Lawrence was not received like that, despite going to jail at least five times in his almost four years of student life in Chandigarh.

Thereon, unlike the older generation of Punjab dons—Dimpy Chandbhan in the 90s, Rocky Fazilka in the 2000s—Lawrence did not keep things local. They had limited influence—occasional extortions in Uttar Pradesh, Maharashtra, maybe a liquor racket or two in Punjab. Lawrence thought bigger. He wanted a criminal multinational. And he made one.

By the early 2020s, his name had entered police files across continents. The Indian security establishment was stunned by the scale. The National Investigation Agency's 2023 chargesheet read like a dossier on a warlord. Lawrence had over 700 operatives, with 300 active in Punjab. His gang maintained 2,500 safe houses across India, from slum tenements to elite condos. His communications used encrypted messaging apps and deep-fake IDs. The network spanned Canada, UK, Germany, Italy, Thailand, the Middle East, and allegedly maintained links to Pakistan's ISI.

◆

It started with Bollywood. When news broke of Salman Khan's alleged blackbuck poaching, the Bishnoi community rose in fury. For them, the blackbuck wasn't just sacred—it was a protector, a symbol of their 15th-century spiritual code. Lawrence, invoking that ancestral fire, threatened Salman's life. It was the first time the media heard his voice. And he wasn't bluffing.

Meanwhile, his syndicate drilled deeper into Punjab and Mumbai. Extortions ran on autopilot. Calls were made from jails. Payments collected via *hawala*. Pollywood and Bollywood figures received ultimatums wrapped in silence. Resistance was brief, if at all.

On 29 May 2022, the murder of Sidhu Moosewala—executed with military precision—shook the nation. The gunmen used GPS tracking, AK-47s, and military-style diversionary tactics. Within hours, Lawrence's gang claimed credit.

Then came the global trail of blood. On 18 June 2023, Hardeep Singh Nijjar, a Khalistan activist based in Surrey, was killed outside a gurdwara. The Canadian government pointed a finger at the Indian intelligence, but another name lay buried in the chatter—Lawrence's syndicate. Ottawa cited intelligence linking Lawrence, through his Canadian arm, to the strike. Even the most hardened investigators admitted that no one moved as fast. Lawrence's lieutenants operated under layers—Goldy Brar in Canada, Lakhbir Landa in Dubai, Rohit Godara in Rajasthan. The syndicates included Kala Jatheri in Delhi-NCR, Jaggu Bhagwanpuria in Punjab. The body count of their turf war with rivals like Sukhpreet Budda and Lucky Patial has crossed 20 since 2015. Their bullets still don't pause.

The Bishnoi Syndicate: A Crime Network across Borders

In the shadowy corridors of North India's criminal underworld, Lawrence Bishnoi emerged as a central figure—an inmate whose influence extended far beyond prison walls. From his cell, Lawrence orchestrated a sprawling syndicate that operated across Punjab, Haryana, Delhi, Rajasthan, Uttar Pradesh, and Chandigarh. His network, built on alliances with other notorious gangsters, was responsible for a range of organized crimes: contract killings, extortions, arms trafficking, land grabs, and high-stakes robberies.

At the heart of the syndicate's operations was a clear hierarchy. Lawrence, along with his Canada-based associate Goldy Brar (separated now), assigned roles and coordinated activities with precision. Even while lodged in separate jails, the key members remained in constant communication. This coordination was evident in the killing of Punjabi singer Sidhu Moosewala. Despite being held in six different prisons, the accused managed to plan and execute the murder after Moosewala's security was downgraded—an operation allegedly greenlit by Goldy after consulting with Lawrence and others behind bars.

Lawrence's reach was amplified through strategic alliances. In Haryana, he partnered with Sandeep alias Kala Jatheri and

Virender Pratap alias Kala Rana. In Delhi, he aligned with Jitender Maan Gogi; in Rajasthan, with Anandpal. His protégé, Anuradha Choudhary—known as Revolver Rani—became a key member of the syndicate. These partnerships allowed Lawrence to maintain control and spread his influence, even while being incarcerated.

The gang's financial operations were equally calculated. Money from extortion, arms smuggling, and illegal liquor trade was funnelled through hawala networks. In 2019, Bishnoi was introduced to Manish Bhandari, a Delhi native based in Thailand, who allegedly laundered the gang's earnings through a chain of nightclubs and restaurants. Bhandari provided shelter and logistical support to gang members during their stay in Thailand, further establishing the syndicate's international footprint.

Funds also flowed to Canada, where Goldy Brar and another associate, Satbir Singh alias Sam, allegedly used the money to finance films, purchase yachts, and sponsor events like the Canadian Premier League. Lawrence admitted to receiving funds from both men to carry out targeted killings and other criminal acts.

Social media played a crucial role in shaping the gang's image. Lawrence's photos from court appearances, often shared online, helped build a cult-like following. Platforms like Instagram and YouTube buzzed with reels showing him like a star.

What began as a regional gang evolved into a transnational syndicate—one that blurred the lines between crime, celebrityhood, and digital influence. The NIA's chargesheet paints a picture not just of a criminal enterprise, but of a network that adapted to modern tools while being rooted in old-school violence and intimidation.

How come a man who swears by vegetarianism and non-violence as taught by the community he was born into became head of an international syndicate to mercilessly order killings?

His uncle, Ramesh, says: 'When pride is at stake, a Bishnoi will strike. Like anyone else.'

The last word on Lawrence is yet to be heard. Back in Dutaranwali, the air is heavy. A police officer who visited his home described it: Lawrence's father is motionless on the sofa, eyes locked to the ground. His mother sobs but is silent. 'They don't talk. They just grieve,' he said.

Their only hope? Both their sons will be back home some day and play cricket or something in the large courtyard or the lawn, or plough the fields driving a tractor.

Their greatest fear—lives fuelled by gunfire end in a hail of bullets. There is a bullet somewhere which may have Lawrence's name on it. In the case of most gangsters, the question is not *whether* this will happen. It is a matter of *when*.

Epilogue

The gangster stories in this book capture the raw fury of Punjab's underworld—ruthless lives marked by ambition, betrayal, and bloodshed. Yet these stories do not end in these pages; the saga surges on, more volatile than ever.

Yesterday's fringe figures have morphed into a hydra-headed threat, entwined with politics, transnational crime, and radical echoes. New faces emerge with unsettling regularity. Punjab today faces a gangster onslaught in which old vendettas fuel fresh violence, extortion, and upheaval. What were once localized rivalries have hardened into a sophisticated criminal ecosystem, testing both law enforcement and societal resolve.

The Lawrence Bishnoi gang has come to spur high-profile hits and sprawling rackets. But 2025 brought a seismic rupture. A split with long-time ally Goldy Brar—reportedly over Anmol Bishnoi's arrest in the US and disputes over control—fractured the syndicate into warring factions. Brar, believed to be living in Canada, distanced himself from Bishnoi, setting the stage for intensified conflict.

Gang wars scar Punjab's streets.

Towards the end of 2025, the Punjab Police released chilling data on their crackdown against gangsters. The figures revealed that since April 2022—when the AGTF was conceived—police had conducted 324 encounters, resulting in the neutralization of 24 dreaded criminals and the arrest of 515 others, DGP Gaurav Yadav disclosed.

'Of the 515 gangsters arrested during encounters, 319 sustained bullet injuries. Three police personnel laid down their lives and 41 others were injured while neutralizing the threat posed by these criminals,' the DGP said on record.

But it was not enough.

In December 2025, Bishnoi ally Inderpreet Singh, alias Perry, was killed in a daylight attack in Chandigarh's Sector 26. Weeks later, kabaddi promoter Kunwar Digvijay Singh, known as Rana Balachauria, was shot dead in Mohali. The killing was claimed by gangster Doni Bal's crew as retribution for allegedly sheltering Sidhu Moosewala's killers. The police denied the claim, but Moosewala's 2022 murder continues to cast a long shadow.

Doni Bal's Devinder Bambiha-linked group has since risen rapidly, allegedly backed from abroad, carrying out extortions and targeted attacks against Bishnoi rivals—signalling the possibility of an all-out gang war. In an unsettling escalation, rival gangsters killed the mother of Category-A gangster Jaggu Bhagwanpuria—the first known instance of a gangster's family member being targeted in this manner.

The profiles in this book reveal how many gangsters emerged from election politics. Yet, years later, the impact of gangsters on elections—and the public's response to active and former gangsters—has become an issue that demands deeper reflection.

Various by-elections, along with Zila Parishad and Panchayat Samiti polls in 2025, highlighted the role of gangsterism in complex and often contradictory ways.

In Ferozepore, voters elected the wife and allies of gangster-turned-reformist Gurpreet Sekhon in local polls. At the same time, people also backed outspoken anti-gang crusaders, revealing a deeply divided electorate. In Apra village in Doaba, BSP candidate Manjit Singh Thekedar won on the strength of his work against gangsters. His cousin, Ram Sarup, was killed by gangsters in 2018, and since then the family has endured sustained threats aimed at silencing their pursuit of justice.

In the Tarn Taran Assembly constituency, which borders the international boundary with Pakistan, the influence of gangsters remained a persistent talking point. An Akali candidate was accused and arrested for alleged links with gangsters. It was also alleged that jailed gangster Jaggu Bhagwanpuria was used by another political party. A senior district police chief was suspended for failing to take timely action against gangsters.

The year 2026 began with a renewed resolve from the Punjab Police. DGP Gaurav Yadav announced that the year would witness the strongest-ever operations against organized crime.

Acknowledgements

This book would not have been possible without the generous support, encouragement, and patience of many individuals and institutions—especially my organization, The Tribune Trust, which stood by me through the long and often turbulent creative pursuits.

I am profoundly grateful to Ms Jyoti Malhotra, Editor-in-Chief of *The Tribune*, who encouraged me to tell the story of Punjab's complex and disturbing modern gangster landscape through the life stories of ten significant figures. I am equally thankful to Mr Sanjeev Singh Bariana, Chief of Bureau at *The Tribune*, whose constant support has been a source of strength throughout this journey.

My literary agent, Ms Jaya Bhattacharji Rose of Ace Literary Consultancy, has been an unfailing pillar of support—reading, critiquing, and patiently helping shape both the book proposal and the manuscript through its many avatars.

At Rupa Publications, I owe an enormous debt of gratitude to my editors, Ms Anupama Roy and Mr Dibakar Ghosh. Their extraordinary patience with my repeatedly missed deadlines, their calm acceptance of last-minute changes, additions, and reorganizations, and their professionalism throughout have been nothing short of remarkable.

My wife, Ms Kanchan Vasdev (Senior Assistant Editor, *The Indian Express*), a journalist of exceptional calibre in her own right, has been my unwavering support. She endured my long absences, unpredictable moods, and the general chaos that comes with living with someone immersed in writing a book of this nature.

Special thanks are due to author and lawyer Sonia Chauhan for her invaluable insights and advice.

I must also place on record my appreciation for the many journalists—especially Yadwinder Karfew, Ritesh Lakhi, Vikram Jit Singh, Simranjot Singh Makkar, Lankesh Trikha, Tejpreet Singh Gill, Arvind Ojha, and Baljeet Parmar—who have produced hundreds of YouTube episodes, interviews, podcasts, and deep-dive stories on Punjab's gangsters. Their tireless work in documenting diverse narratives, claims, counter-claims, and folk versions of these lives has been an important resource and reference point.

Finally, my most sincere thanks go to the Punjab Police and various central security agencies who, despite their enormous pressures and responsibilities, found time to share insights, explain operational challenges, and help me understand how these most-wanted criminals were eventually tracked and apprehended. But for the courage, professionalism, and tireless work of these brave officers, far more blood would have been spilled on the roads of Punjab.

To everyone named—and to the many others who helped in ways big and small—thank you. This book is as much yours as it is mine.

Bibliography

'Achievements', *Online Bangalore*, https://tinyurl.com/4ht4kdmb. Accessed on 3 December 2025.

'BADP Ferozpur: Draft Report', *Government of Punjab*, https://tinyurl.com/4t2km7d6. Accessed on 3 December 2025.

Chaudhry, Amrita, 'Notorious Criminal Escapes from Custody; Two Cops Injured', *The Indian Express*, 30 January 2009, https://tinyurl.com/my9cyj4v. Accessed on 3 December 2025.

Chhina, Gurpreet Singh, 'Chandigarh Was Where Rocky Cut His Teeth into Crime', *Hindustan Times*, 2 May 2016, https://tinyurl.com/2s3c3hwa. Accessed on 3 December 2025.

Divyansh, 'From 1977 to 2017: How Student Politics Changed Over the Years at Panjab University', *Hindustan Times*, 6 September 2017, https://tinyurl.com/axvp9372. Accessed on 3 December 2025.

'Fazilka Gangster-Turned-Politician Shot Dead', *The Tribune*, 1 May 2016, https://tinyurl.com/3r5yauwe. Accessed on 3 December 2025.

'Gangster Caught in Faridkot', *Hindustan Times*, 6 March 2015, https://tinyurl.com/v7t2wuwm. Accessed on 3 December 2025.

Garg, Balwant, 'Proceedings Begin for Transit Remand of Gangster', *The Times of India*, 11 October 2004, https://tinyurl.com/5fbxmsyy. Accessed on 3 December 2025.

Mann, Gurdeep Singh, 'Judicial Remand for Gangster Shera's Moll', *The Tribune*, 9 September 2012, https://tinyurl.com/7zwrvwab. Accessed on 3 December 2025.

Mann, Gurdeep Singh, 'Judicial remand for Gangster Shera's moll', *The Tribune*, 9 September 2012, https://tinyurl.com/7zwrvwab. Accessed on 3 December 2025.

'Nabha Jail' ਚ ਰਾਤ ਕੱਟਕੇ ਆਏ Gurpreet Sekhon ਦਾ Interview MLA ਨਾਲ ਮੁਟੇ ਕਿਓਂ ਫਸੀ ਗਰਾਰੀ, MLA ਨੂੰ ਚੈਲੰਜ [Interview with Gurpreet Sekhon after Spending a Night in Nabha Jail: Hear Why Matters Escalated, a Challenge to the MLA]', *YouTube*, https://tinyurl.com/3d8t436z. Accessed on 5 January 2026.

'No Headway in Rocky Murder Case', *The Tribune*, 24 August 2016, https://tinyurl.com/54rr9tyh. Accessed on 3 December 2025.

Pande, Alka, 'A Slice of Sicily', *Outlook India*, 19 December 2005, archived at https://tinyurl.com/4pfezfus. Accessed on 3 December 2025.

Prashar, Saurabh, 'Crime Branch Has Arrested a Notorious Arms Smuggler Ranjit Singh Dhillon, Alias Dupla', *The Times of India*, 13 December 2011, https://tinyurl.com/55fk4hu7. Accessed on 3 December 2025.

'Rocky Murder: Jailed Gangsters Take Shots on FB', *The Times of India*, 2 May 2016, https://tinyurl.com/ahb625wu. Accessed on 3 December 2025.

Sharma, Sachin, 'Gangster-Politician Rocky Killed: Rivals Celebrate "Revenge" on Facebook', *Hindustan Times*, 30 April 2016, https://tinyurl.com/4a5krsa3. Accessed on 3 December 2025.

Singh, Manmeet, 'Murder Suspect Gives Cops the Slip', *The Times of India*, 29 January 2009, https://tinyurl.com/5e3svmxy. Accessed on 3 December 2025.

Verma, Sharat K., 'City Police May Bring Rajiv Raja to Ludhiana on Production Warrants', *The Indian Express*, 8 June 2009, https://tinyurl.com/d3ja2kn4. Accessed on 3 December 2025.

'Vicky Gounder ਦੇ ਸਾਥੀ Neeta Deol ਨਾਲ Exclusive Podcast. ਸੁਣੋ ਕਿੱਦਾਂ ਮਾ.ਰਿਆ ਵਿੱਕੀ ਗੌਂਡਰ? [Exclusive Podcast with Vicky Gounder's Associate Neeta Deol: Hear How Vicky Gounder Was Killed]', *YouTube*, https://tinyurl.com/33kmjurv. Accessed on 5 December 2025.

'ਸ਼ਾਨਦਾਰ ਜਿੱਤ ਤੋਂ ਬਾਅਦ Gurpreet Sekhon ਦੀ Exclusive Interview LIVE, ਗੱਲਾਂ ਕਰਦਿਆਂ ਦੇ ਅੱਖਾਂ 'ਚੋਂ ... [Exclusive Live Interview with Gurpreet Sekhon after a Magnificent Victory; Emotions Well Up While Speaking...]', *YouTube*, https://tinyurl.com/bbcfpscn. Accessed on 5 January 2026.

'ਪੁਲਿਸ ਨੇ ਸ਼ੇਰੇ ਖੁੱਬਣ ਨੂੰ ਬੁਰੀ ਤਰਾਂ ਕੁੱਟਿਆ, ਜੈਪਾਲ ਸਹਾਰਾ ਦੇਕੇ 3 ਨੰਬਰ ਬੈਰਕ 'ਚ ਲੈਕੇ ਆਇਆ | Sonu Bajwa [Police Brutally Beat Shere Khubban; Jaipal Gave Support and Brought Him to Barrack No. 3]', *YouTube*, https://tinyurl.com/4b5t8zmb. Accessed on 5 January 2026.